Job and the Mystery of Suffering

"Job was struck down with sores from the sole of his foot to the top of his head. He took a potsherd to scrape his wounds and sat among the ashes." (JOB 2:7–8)

"I have not turned away. I have offered my back to those who struck me, my cheeks to those who plucked my beard; I have not turned my face away from insult and spitting." (ISA. 50:5–6)

"He is destined to be opposed, and you yourself [Mary] *will be pierced by a sword so that the secret thoughts of many will be laid bare."* (LUKE 2:34–35)

"He had no form or charm to attract us, no beauty to win our hearts, he was despised, the lowest of men, a man of sorrows, familiar with suffering, one from whom we averted our gaze." (ISA. 53:2–3)

"And slapping him in the face . . . they brought out Jesus wearing a crown of thorns. . . . And Pilate said, 'Behold the man!' " (JOHN 19:3, 5)

The wounded one is the gift giver

RICHARD ROHR

Job and the Mystery of Suffering

SPIRITUAL REFLECTIONS

A Crossroad Book
The Crossroad Publishing Company
New York

This printing: 2004

The Crossroad Publishing Company
16 Penn Plaza, 481 Eighth Avenue, New York, NY 10001

Printed in the United States of America

Library of Congress Cataloging-in-Publication Data

Rohr, Richard.
Job and the mystery of suffering / Richard Rohr.
p. cm.
ISBN 0-8245-1474-2; 0-8245-1734-2 (pbk.)
1. Bible. O.T. Job – Devotional literature. 2. Suffering – Biblical teaching. 3. Suffering – Religious aspects – Christianity. I. Title.
BS1415.4.R64 1996
223'106–dc20 96-10348
CIP

For all the victims
and scapegoats of human history,
who never had a chance,
with trust that there is an answer
in the voice from the whirlwind.

Contents

Preface

VIRGINIA WOOLF, in her postmodern novel *The Waves*, speaks through the character of Bernard, who searches for his truth through words and ideas. He never allows himself to find that truth and remains a professional skeptic and unbeliever, an image of the modern self. Bernard substitutes storytelling for any serious commitment to a larger self. Yet he still holds on to some hidden hope that there is a "true story" out there which will hold all reality together.

I think Job is the "true story" that both Woolf and contemporary society are seeking. It is the perennial "ungodly" story that must be told whenever God makes no sense and we are tempted to tell stories other than the story of faith. If there is no story that reveals beforehand the essentially tragic (but triumphant) nature of human life, we had best be prepared for a cynical, resentful, and violent history. Perhaps we are already there. Consider the words of Bernard as a near prophecy of our Western culture today:

> I have made up thousands of stories; I have filled innumerable notebooks with phrases to be used when I found the true story, the one to which all these phrases refer. But I have never found that story... I, who am always distracted, at once make up a story and so obliterate the angles of the crucifix.

But we have found that story here. The Book of Job is not a "made-up" story of distracted people, but a story painfully rediscovered and repeated by all peoples of faith. Nowhere is it told with greater daring and brilliance than in this unlikely and enduring tale of biblical faith.

In this book of the Hebrew and Christian scriptures I believe biblical revelation reaches both its summit and its dead end. Perhaps this is why it is quoted rather rarely, why it is not commonly a subject for religious artists (except for William Blake's magnificent drawings), and why it is almost unknown by the mass of the faithful. The Book of Job is too much for almost all of us. It moves us beyond words and appropriate theologies into a luminous darkness that refuses to "obliterate the angles of the crucifix."

Job called it "the voice from the whirlwind"; Jesus called it "the sign of Jonah"; Augustine called it "the paschal mystery"; and Christians call it "the cross." It seems to be the quintessential religious story, and we are going to try to enter this luminous darkness in the following pages.

It is the true story and the same story as that of Jeremiah and Julian of Norwich, the same pattern discovered by Simone Weil, Anne Frank, Mohandas Gandhi, and Nelson Mandela. It is the answer beyond and before all answers, the nonresolution that resolves everything. Before the death and resurrection of Jesus, Job lived and died and lived the same liberating path unto God.

We would have to deny all our heroes and heroines, we would have to reject the "voice from the whirlwind," we would have to oppose what we already know, if we were to doubt that this dark path of descent is also the preeminent path of all great religions, and surely the path of Jesus.

Acknowledgments

I want to thank Michael Farrell for turning these taped talks into book form. Without his patience, caring, and skill, these words would never have become flesh. My own Holy Spirit!

I also want to thank Patricia Karg, whose evocative drawings are found throughout the book. We met "by chance" after a lecture in Austria, and she offered me these recent artworks for inclusion here. An infusion of soul, as you will see.

Finally, I want to thank Michael Leach and Bob Heller at Crossroad, who have continued to support and encourage my work, but even more have supported *me* through my own Job periods.

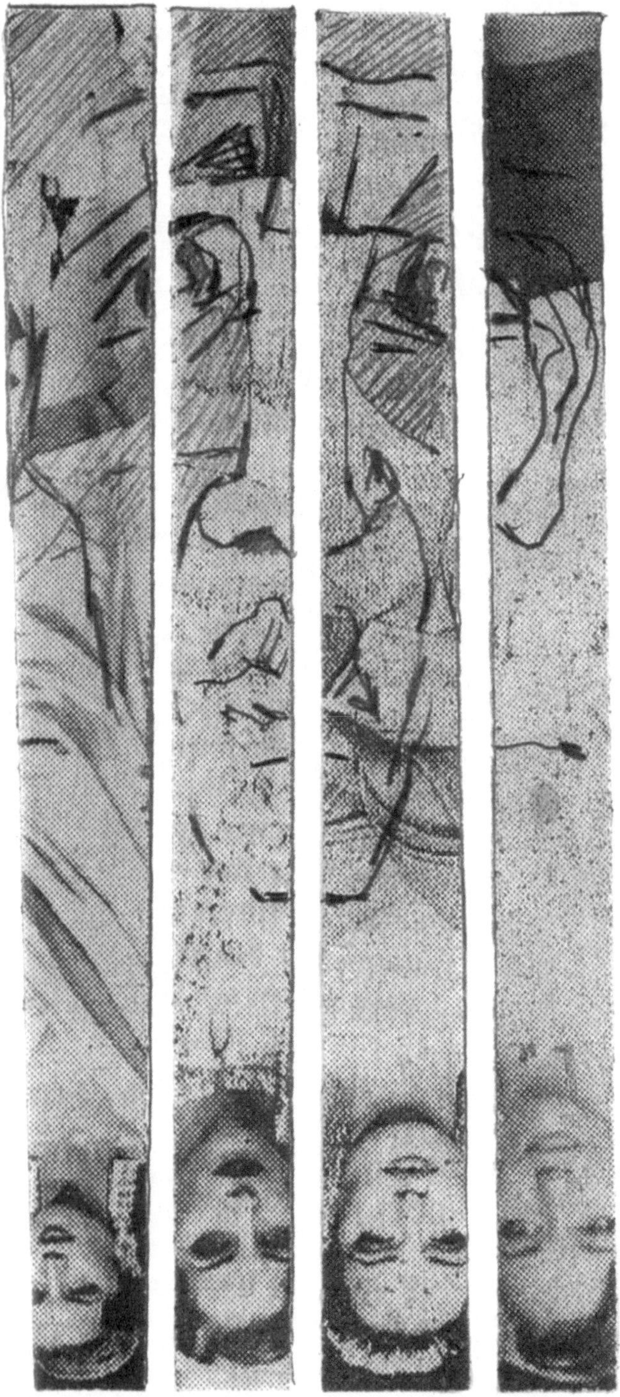

Chapter 1

A Story of Conversion

ALTHOUGH THE JOB STORY has usually been regarded as a study of the mystery of evil — and it is — I'd prefer to look at it as the anatomy of a conversion. For later generations it might be described as a postgraduate course in moral education. For every age it is the diagram for those who "fall into the hands of the living God" (Heb. 10:31).

If we view it as a journey into an ever-deepening encounter with God, this will keep it from becoming an abstract debate observed from a distance. We can't observe the question of suffering from a distance. Unless we've felt it, unless we've been up against the wall, at a place where, frankly, God doesn't make sense anymore, the Book of Job is probably going to be only an academic study.

A big obstacle to authentic Christianity is that so much of it has been only secondhand knowledge. All too often, the word of God comes to us as follows: "This is what the church says about God.... This is what priests say about God.... This is what the Bible says about God." All that is insufficient evidence. "Hearsay" knowledge has little power, as Job himself will finally recognize (42:5).

Hand-me-down Christianity can be interesting. It may allow us to answer the questions of suffering friends a little faster, but the answers will be glib, tripping off our tongue. "We know you've lost your child, but we know he's up in heaven now" — that is a sufficient answer only for a person who hasn't lost a child.

When we are truly bereaved, expressions like "God has a bigger plan" fall flat. True, but all wrong. Mouthing such a platitude is sometimes premature when all we want to do, as Job wanted to do, is curse God.

All the catechism answers we've been given in our years of religious training and all our Bible studies don't mean much at such times. Unless we find the grace to put ourselves in the sufferer's place, if circumstances have not put us there already, our reactions will be empty academic answers.

I ask the reader to pray for me, because, not having suffered a great deal, I don't know whether I have earned the right to teach about Job. I have had a rather easy life. Despite my claim that there must be a lived experience, most of what I have to share is only what I learned from theology. (This is much less true at the age of fifty-two when these teachings are being put in book form than when I first spoke them to an audience. Now I can say that suffering has both formed and informed me.)

But I have also learned from other great teachers, suffering people and suffering societies. I refer not only to individuals who feel like cursing God because of all they've endured, yet go on believing. I also refer to the corporate evil in the world today, our seemingly insurmountable social problems, which nevertheless produce creativity and endless compassion. The people who don't have answers, yet survive, seem to be the Jobs of every age.

In America I have learned from individual suffering and heroic lives. In other countries I have learned from whole peoples who have embodied suffering and resurrection. People "on the top" are slow learners, which is one of the reasons any "established" church is hard to preach to. People "on the bottom" have a symbolic head start toward truth.

It helps to have suffered

It's hard even to understand the Bible because we don't come from a situation of persecution. And the vast majority of us don't come from a situation of poverty, oppression, enslavement, or marginalization, which is the privileged perspective for a "beginner's mind." There's a certain way the Gospel is heard when one's stomach is empty. And a very different way it is heard when a people is satisfied.

The Gospel was first heard by people who were longing and thirsty, who were poor and oppressed in one sense or another. They knew their need and their emptiness.

It's pointless to pray, "Lord, put me in a situation of oppression." But we must go inside and find the rejected and fearful parts within each of us and try to live there if life has not yet put us there. That should allow us a deeper communion with the oppressed of the world, who are by far the majority of the human race. We are the minority, the exception, the slow learners.

If we wish to enter more deeply into this mystery of redemptive suffering, which also means somehow entering more deeply into the heart of God, we have to ask the Lord to allow us to feel, not just to know. To feel what it means to be empty, abandoned, uncared for. Not only for five minutes and not only about trivia like missing the bus, but rather, an entire life's stance, a standing-under, so that we can "understand." This change of position is what we mean by "conversion." *Metanoia* means turning around. It's quite different from mere education.

Divine grace under pressure

Working with the peace movement in Germany some years ago, I visited what was then East Germany. On the other side of the Wall, I experienced a purified Christianity. If you were going to identify yourself as a Christian there, you had to ask real questions, because you were going to pay a price. As soon as you put your name on the docket as a believer or attended a religious service, you knew you were not going to get certain promotions.

As a result, the church was in no way as big as in West

Germany, but it was an authentic church. Maybe that's what the Lord is leading us to — a smaller church of conviction, a community of faith that has walked the journey of Job — and now lives according to a new pattern.

So Job is not just individuals we've all met. There is also a corporate Job, a whole people who have been up against the wall. Sometimes groups embody the same struggle for faith we're going to encounter in this book.*

Why do the joints stiffen, people ask. Why do sensible plans go nonsensically off course? Why do the innocent suffer? Why are there genetic defects in newborn children? Why have so many died before they had a chance to live? If God is good, why is there so much that seems ungood? We're going to walk around that mystery in this book.

Religious education has for years given people answers to questions they're not asking. The people accept the answers quickly and easily. And the answers go about an inch deep. And the people, all too often, spout the answers for the rest of their lives. "God is the Supreme Being who made all things," or whatever else it might be.

But such knowledge can pass away as quickly as it came, because we never thirsted for it. Until we make space inside, what comes is not an answer but an excuse — an excuse not to face the question, an excuse to stop searching, to avoid the journey.

There's too much cultural Christianity all about us. It's rather innocuous, but it's often more the problem than the answer. Many people are no longer on a journey. They have easy Christian answers before they have struggled with the question. Such Christianity has not dealt with the folly of the cross.

The dying one who shouldn't be dying is always the acid test: What happens when life doesn't work? What happens when it's not enough to wave our hands at a prayer meeting or kneel at a Mass? How do we believe then? That

*See Gustavo Gutiérrez, *On Job* (Orbis, 1984).

is the question of the Book of Job. The questions of Job prepare people for the stunning mystery of the cross. Paul explained that the crucifixion of Christ could not be expressed in philosophical terms. Not philosophy but praxis.

Thorns on the rose

If we didn't deal very well with Job, we probably won't deal well with Jesus Christ. The mystery of why there are thorns on the rose eventually becomes a question of who God is. We can glibly say that God is good, God is merciful, kind and faithful. But a great many people on earth can say, "I don't have any evidence for that. Maybe you do, but I don't."

And even in America, for all our wealth, there are myriad individual lives of suffering and poverty. Were we honest, maybe many of us would admit we do not have a lot of conviction about God's goodness either.

For some people, faith seems to be whistling in the dark, hoping against hope that God is indeed good. But in brutally honest moments they're not sure they believe or feel it. They may want to. That's a beginning, and a work of grace, and one should not dismiss it. It may be the path for many. We may begin by whistling in the dark, but that isn't faith yet.

Faith is a unique creation of both grace and freedom. It's a choice we become capable of by God's love. "A mysterious meeting of two freedoms," Gutiérrez calls it. A freedom that God is and a freedom that we must become.

The rabbinic tradition relates the story of a young fugitive who comes to a town where the people are willing to take him in and hide him. When soldiers arrive in search of the fugitive, the townspeople protest that they know nothing. Suspecting their lie, the soldiers warn that, unless the fugitive is turned over by morning, the entire town will be destroyed.

In deep fear the people rush to their pastor for counsel. The priest, greatly troubled, starts searching scripture for an answer. All night he reads and finds nothing. Then, just before dawn, his eyes fall on a passage, "It is better that one man should die for the people than that the whole people be lost."

He is sure that's the answer, and goes to the people with the news. The soldiers are informed that the fugitive is indeed hidden among them, and the young man is taken away. They throw a big party in the town, lasting far into the night, and celebrate their deliverance by the grace of God.

But the pastor returns to his study, still troubled. An angel appears to him and asks what's his problem. "I still don't feel right about turning over the fugitive," the pastor says. The angel replies, "Did you not know that he was the Messiah?"

The pastor is incredulous. "How was I to know?" he asks. "If, instead of reading your Bible," the angel replies, "you had taken time to visit the young man and looked into his eyes, you would have known he was the Messiah."

When we separate the scriptures from history, we are in trouble. When we separate the scriptures from real life, we distort the scriptures. When we separate the scriptures from the people out of whom the scriptures were written, we misinterpret the scriptures.

The Lord entered history. And ever after, history and the flesh are where we encounter the Lord, rather than running from life and history into principles, theories, and the too-quick answers that put us back in control.

How to handle scripture

Nothing in the New Testament says the primary authority is the scriptures themselves. Scriptural authority rests in pointing beyond itself to history, to what-is, to God. When we make an idol of the book, when we make an end of the words themselves, we get into trouble, as the pastor did in the story.

The point of scripture is to do the very thing that the writers of scripture did, that Moses and Abraham did: go out on the journey and there meet the Lord. And then continually come back to the word of God for confirmation and hopefully consolation.

Jesus told his religious leaders that they "knew how to read the face of the sky but they could not read the signs of the times" (Matt. 16:3). If we are not a listening people, if we're not an open people, a discerning people, a humble people, we're not going to find much truth. We're simply going to have our scripture passages. Then, instead of an avenue to God, or a window, the scriptures become a barrier. Or even an end in themselves.

That same phrase used in the fugitive story was used by Caiaphas the high priest in justifying the death of the original Messiah: "It is better that one man should die than that the whole people should perish" (John 18:14).

The perennial temptation is to scapegoat rather than to carry the dark side of things. Demonizing the other makes us feel superior and "saved." We compromise the Gospel for the purposes of group solidarity or good management. It is much easier to belong to a group than to belong to God. To belong to a group one usually has to be convinced the group is "right"; to belong to God, one always knows one is as wrong as everybody else. They are two very different journeys.

It is exciting to discover that, all over the world, the church is coming to recognize that we can't compromise the Gospel any longer. We can't use it to support particular cultures, to sustain the myths and prejudices of individual countries or denominations. Jesus has already been sacrificed too often so that people can legitimate their fears and prejudices. To "kill a commie for Christ" is an oxymoron.

The faith of Job as we are going to study it will deter us from doing that. We have to face our fears and doubts from page one. An awful lot of religion is an excuse for not facing our fears and doubts. True religion is not denial but transformation.

God walks with us into our fears, to feel them, to own

them, to let them teach us. We need to say, "I'm afraid, Lord, how do I deal with this fear?" We tell God we're hurting and life is falling apart. We've lost a job or a loved one, and we don't know how to believe, hope, or love.

Faith cannot rest. Faith definitions grow old as we move through our lives. Periodically we have to say, "Lord, what does faith mean now?" This isn't easy. Yet, God is patient, it seems, and knows that most of us grow slowly. Although the common phrase has been "the patience of Job," we will see in this story that Job is actually very *impatient* and it is, in fact, a story of *God's* patience and love for Job.

Job's new skin

So God may let us plateau for a while, say, between thirty and forty — "we'll let you just sit there with your satisfying definition of faith." Then God throws us a whammy or a double whammy to get us to go further. If he doesn't, we won't move outside our comfort zone. Unless we're kicked or pulled or shoved, we all take the path of least resistance — understandably. Life is hard enough; why would we make it harder on ourselves?

We won't move, ordinarily, until the old answers don't work any more. Pain is an activator that forces us to choose between what is important and what is not.

Scientists say that every seven years we acquire all new skin and cells and we're constantly regenerating. It also seems that more than our cells change: It's just about every seven years that the old answers don't work any more. Some say no, it's every two years. Or one. But give or take a few years, every so often, it doesn't work. If, at forty-two, you're still using your fourteen-year-old answers, my reaction is that you're not growing. And I'm afraid that's a lot of the Christianity we have in the West. Childish more than childlike.

I found much more of that in West Berlin than in East

Berlin, as they were then called. There was no room for that kind of Christianity in East Berlin. But West Berlin was filled with it: churches filled with happy, singing people — and almost no commitment.

I grew up being told that communism was atheistic materialism, and that's an understandable definition, but I saw a lot more materialism in West Berlin than in East Berlin. The communism I saw was only a fraction as materialistic as I see in our own country.

I was also told the East Germans were atheists and we were not. There was indeed a terrible official atheism. But the Christianity I met was real Christianity, and what I very often meet in our world is just practical atheism hiding behind the trappings of Christianity.

Which is worse? They both have to be challenged. That's the power of the word of God — it challenges all systems. And it is subject to none. That's what the pope has been saying for several years on his travels.

The trouble with so many of us is that we opt to stand in one little system — the American system or the Roman Catholic system or the Christian system or the white middle-class system — and stand in it justified and self-assured. We think we have all the answers, but we're not very wise. The word of God calls us to greater wisdom.

The only way the Lord can do so is *by making the system fall apart.* That's called suffering. It's how God shows us that life is always bigger than we presently imagine it. Faith allows us deliberately to live in a shaky position so that we *have* to rely upon Another. God gets closer blow by blow.

That's why the Gospel needs to be preached so hard in our country. More than any people on the face of the earth, we are able to buy our way out of faith. Many of us are able to avoid it until late in life. It's only in old age, when the body begins to rot on us, that many of us experience that we're not in charge. Meanwhile, we can maintain the illusion (longer than anyone else!) of living in an infinite world with endless options.

A young married man in East Berlin, a profound Christian, said to me: "You have a lot of options in your country that you can choose from. Freedom for you seems to be a world of preferences, choices, and options. But we're not sure that you've discovered true freedom at all. From our perspective you're not doing any of your thousand options very well. Here, we may have only five options, and so we have to do a few things well. That forces us to enter the inner reality and access the spiritual resources there. I'm not sure that our inner freedom isn't stronger than yours."

And I have to say I was not sure either. Many of us *have* to do what we *want* to do (the addictive society); whereas many "limited" people have learned how to *want* to do what they *have* to do (true freedom).

Religion is not enough

It is only in situations like that of Job that we create and maintain and purify faith and freedom. Otherwise, faith becomes largely a matter of religion. I'm not interested in religion any more. Religion has been the cause of as much damage on this earth as good. Religion has been used to justify almost all the wars in the history of humanity. It's been used to justify racial prejudice in South Africa, for example. The whole system of apartheid was maintained by theology and the scriptures.

South African religion was able to co-opt a vague scriptural image for its own immoral purposes. This religion, in effect, said: The rainbow is a sign of the covenant (Gen. 9:13–16). If the colors were not separate, there would be no rainbow. So God intends the separation of the colors, and it is our job as ministers to see that the colors stay separate. That's what happens when the scriptures are used by unconverted people.

Every oppressive, lethal system on earth will find a theology to back it up. It was interesting, in Germany, to see the belt buckles worn in two world wars: "*Gott mit uns,*" God is with us, was written on them. Hitler frequently quoted the scriptures. One must have God in one's system or there is no way to sacralize the needed violence. The communists were at least honest enough not to pretend God was in their system. Almost everybody else does.

Is Jesus your "personal lord and savior"? This phrase has become very popular, even though it's very recent, and very individualistic. I get letters every week from people telling me they have made Jesus their lord and savior. I'm glad they have, but it's going to take most of us all our lives to know what that means.

"If he is your lord and savior, why are you looking for salvation in money?" I ask some of my friends. If Jesus is our savior, why is most of life preoccupied with a job promotion, with getting a second home and then a retirement home? If Jesus is our savior, why are we so militaristic and preoccupied with making more and more bombs? Jesus isn't our savior. Bottom line, the gun is where we put our trust.

To have Jesus as one's lord and savior has to have historical content and concrete meaning. It's not just a concept in our heads, and Jesus dare not be used as a mere totem or mascot for our own personal religion any longer.

It demands moving from the head down to the heart and gut. I don't know whether I, personally, can trust Jesus in that kind of real way. I struggle as much with this as others do. I'm in the middle of it. We all are. Western Christianity is trying desperately to move from theory to practice, as the world discounts our theory because it is so seldom practiced.

Reframing the problem

We will all have a problem similar to Job's so long as we picture God as "the one who does not suffer." Job didn't know about Jesus, of course, so it's easier to excuse his mistake.

But it's amazing that, even after we've seen the incarnation, we Christians fall so readily into the same misconception.

The enfleshment and suffering of Jesus is saying that God is not apart from the trials of humanity. God is not aloof. God is not a mere spectator. God is participating with us.

God is not merely tolerating human suffering. Or healing suffering. God is participating with us *in it.* That is what gives believers both meaning and hope. Paul described it as only a mystic can: "It makes me happy to suffer for you, as I am suffering now, and in my own body to do what I can to make up all that still has to be undergone by Christ for the sake of his body, the church" (Col. 1:24).

This makes a nice line for a sermon — that God is participating in suffering, not just looking on. But we go even further: We seem to believe that this suffering is even life-giving and redemptive. It's quite amazing.

We live in a finite world where everything is dying, shedding its strength. This is hard to accept, and all our lives we look for exceptions to it. We look for something certain, strong, undying, infinite. Religion tells us that something is God. Great, we say, we'll attach ourselves to this strong God. Then this God comes along and says, "Even I suffer. Even I participate in the finiteness of this world."

This concept is echoed throughout the Book of Job, so we need to come to terms with it. Our usual definitions of God depict him omnipotent, infinite, perfect in every way. Yet, if the suffering Jesus is the image and revelation of the invisible God (Col. 1:15), this is totally at odds with all the other philosophical and theological definitions of a supreme being.

Jesus doesn't fit. Even after two thousand years, it is hard to realize what a revolutionary symbol, revelation, and reality Jesus is. He basically turned theology upside down. He said, in effect: Who you think God is, God isn't. You can't know this merely by study or theology or religion, but only through painful encounters with the living God where you feel your flesh being torn off and yet you do not die. Then you experience another kind of life, another kind of freedom.

Christians call it the life of the risen Jesus.

This is the mystery of Jesus. After such an encounter, we can legitimately say, "I've met Jesus. He is my personal lord and savior."

This may explain why the people who have met Jesus are humble people. Because they have been overwhelmed by a humble God. A God who is not overwhelming and triumphant, with all the answers and all the perfection, but a God who is somehow in this with us. A God who is infinite, yet somehow finite. Who is in charge, yet chooses not to be in control at all.

I don't know how, logically, to put these contrary images of God together. But I look at the crucified and raised-up body of Jesus and I meet a collision of opposites that somehow reconciles the paradox. Thus I'm able to arrive at a different name for God. Jesus is the collision of opposites, the different name for God.

Poor Job didn't have the image of Jesus to look at, so he sat on the dung heap and suffered, with no answer except the one emerging within his own flesh. In Job the wonderful revelations of the Jewish scriptures had come to a breaking point, an impasse, a need for a further image, an answer that we could "hear and see and touch" (1 John 1:1). For now, Job himself had become that image that we would later recognize and honor in Jesus.

Jeremiah paving the way

There were other preparations in the Old Testament. If the author of the Book of Job (we don't know who it was) knew any other parts of the Old Testament, it seems most likely that he was familiar with Jeremiah. The Job story was probably written between 500 and 400 B.C.E., that is, after the exile of 587. We know Jeremiah lived before the exile but remained in Palestine after Jerusalem fell.

It is interesting that Israel does not deal with the question of failure and suffering until after the experience of the exile. Most of us don't deal with it until we're in the second half of life. Thus, the earlier writings are all about how Israel can succeed and conquer. They're preoccupied with law and order, structure and identity, the usual concerns of the first part of life.

But Judaism doesn't get purified until during and after the exile, when the whole thing has fallen apart, when all they built up is flattened overnight. The challenge is clear: Now, how do we believe? That's when the greatest Old Testament wisdom emerges. Maybe we are hoping for the same today.

In Jeremiah we see what looks like a direct parallel to Job. In Jeremiah we have the reluctant prophet. He doesn't want to get involved. He feels used. Or, as he says in several places, "raped" and seduced by God: God, you have used me, you have given me a life I didn't want, now I'm so into it there's nothing else I can do, but I still hate it (see Jer. 20:7–18).

The first passage we might characterize as the "confessions" of Jeremiah is taken from the image of temple sacrifice and from Isaiah 53:7: "I, for my part, was like a trustful lamb being led to the slaughterhouse, not knowing the schemes they were plotting against me.... But you, Yahweh Sabaoth, who pronounce a just sentence, who probe the loins and heart, let me see the vengeance you will take on them, for I have committed my cause to you" (11:19–20).

One can see Jeremiah's anger, his desire for revenge. He wants justice against his enemies. Jesus will eventually move beyond this.

Early in Jeremiah 12 we see a question asked that will later be asked in Job: "You have right on your side, Yahweh, when I complain about you." You are always in charge, in other words, you seem to have all the answers. "But I would like to debate a point of justice with you (this already begins to sound like Job): Why is it that the wicked live so prosperously?"

Why are the pagans driving Cadillacs? Why do scoundrels enjoy peace? "You plant them, they take root and flourish, and even bear fruit." They're having, in short, a nice life. Their children are not causing them any trouble, while my daughter is on drugs.

God is always on their lips, Jeremiah complains. Yet, God is far from their hearts. But, on the other hand, "you know me, Yahweh, you see me, you probe my heart, it is in your hands." So, at the end, Jeremiah puts himself, a bit grudgingly, back into the hands of the Lord.

Then he moves back into anger. "Drag them off like sheep for the slaughterhouse, reserve them for the day of butchery." Jeremiah has just the beginnings of freedom. He hasn't arrived there yet. He is always vacillating. For a moment he surrenders to God; then his anger takes over again.

Chapter 15, verses 10–21 of Jeremiah is perhaps the best known of his "confessions," by which we mean his personal lament, his own statement of his relationship to God. "Woe is me, my mother, for you have borne me to be a man of strife and of dissension for all the land. I neither lend nor borrow, yet all of them curse me. Truthfully, Yahweh, have I not done my best to serve you, interceded with you for my enemy in the time of his disaster, his distress? You know I have." It's a personal complaint as old as the ages and as topical as today: I always did the right thing, but where has it gotten me?

In verse 19 we find Yahweh responding to Jeremiah: "If you come back, I will take you back into my service; and if you utter noble, not despicable thoughts, you shall be as my own mouth. They will come back to you, but you must not go back to them. I will make you a bronze wall fortified against this people. They will fight against you, but they will not overcome you, because *I am with you* to save you and to deliver you."

It's the same old wonderful line spoken to all the greats of the Old Testament. The Lord doesn't give them a strategy or a pattern, simply a promise. "I am with you."

The slow collapse of our logic

Chapter 18 of Jeremiah hints at why, even for a prophet, God's word is often hard to swallow: "Listen to me, Yahweh, hear what my adversaries are saying. Should evil be returned for good? For they are digging a pit for me. Remember how I stood in your presence to plead on their behalf, to turn your wrath away from them."

Recall how we feel when we've done the right thing, when maybe we've gone beyond the call of duty. All of us, no matter how purified, have strings attached to the good things we do. We expect something back.

This ethos has never been more obvious than in our own day. It has almost become the Gospel in some American churches: the "prosperity Gospel." We expect blessings and success in return for following Jesus. People could never seriously have read either Jeremiah or Job and certainly do not understand the cross if they believe the Gospel is a promise of success and prosperity in this world.

That is an especially American heresy, and an absolute denial of the teaching of the scriptures. Yet it is being taught widely in so-called "turned-on" Christian churches. If you love Jesus, you'll get better jobs and earn more money. That is not the word of God. It is, in fact, absolutely contrary to the promises of God.

Yet, within human nature, as we see here in Jeremiah, there is something of that expectation. Tit for tat. I'll be nice to you, God, and you be nice to me. We all feel that, but the Bible keeps insisting: No, that's not the way it works. Retributive theology, we will see, is one of the major problems of Job.

Jeremiah 20:7 is probably the most quoted of the confessions. "You have seduced me, Yahweh, and I have let myself be seduced." Jeremiah is upset. "You have overpowered me," one translation goes on. Literally it is, "You have raped me." What an image — raped by God. Jeremiah pictures himself as a helpless woman in relation to God: "I am a daily laughingstock. I am the butt of everybody's joke. Each time I speak the word, I have to howl."

He says elsewhere: "Always I have to proclaim violence and ruin. The word of Yahweh has meant insult and derision all day long." Not exactly a gospel of prosperity and peacefulness.

Jeremiah in 20:9 is very revealing: "I used to say, 'I will not think about him.' " Who of us hasn't felt that way? "I will not speak in his name any more." Then, maybe, he might go away, and I can live a normal life, Jeremiah is thinking.

Then follows the admission: "But then there seemed to be a fire burning in my heart, imprisoned in my bones. The effort to restrain it wearied me. I could not bear it. I hear so many disparaging me, terror coming from every side: 'Denounce him, let us denounce him.' All those who used to be my friends watch for my downfall."

Jeremiah, in all this, was struggling with the same thing that Job would struggle with, that Jesus would struggle with. It's the mystery we're going to struggle with here: How do we believe, how do we trust the love of God when we don't feel love in this world? How do we trust the presence of God when we don't find happiness in this world?

It would be satisfying to end a chapter with some kind of denouement, some resolution. But perhaps the Lord wants us to live with the message of Jeremiah for a while, to taste it, own it, dig down inside ourselves and find that place in our lives that doesn't feel like life at all. Then we will be ready to journey with Job.

Chapter 2

What to Do about Evil

ALTHOUGH THE PATIENCE OF JOB has become a legendary cliché (originating in James 5:10–11), the Book of Job could just as well be called "The Impatience of Job." Impatience, even outrage at God's refusal to do justice, is the primary focus here.

Harold Kushner's excellent book *When Bad Things Happen to Good People* deals with the identical problem. It is a universal dilemma that we are forever forced to confront. We struggle to reconcile a good God with a seemingly evil world. But we are never able to make the answers fit. In the East, some forms of Hinduism and Buddhism have resolved it by a kind of denial, a kind of repression of desire—looking the other way and pretending the bad doesn't happen. It's a rather successful way of dealing with it. Grace has surely worked through these great religions for much of the world. Human beings had to survive through so much pain and disappointment.

Good God, bad things

We can't say God is bad, or we will go nowhere. All religions begin with the assumption that God is good. But then we look at the reality in front of us, and there begins the most unnerving problem: why the just person suffers.

Job is described at the outset as a good and just man. It seems fair to say that this saga does not create Job's faith;

rather, it identifies and names it. His troubles don't make Job into a saint. They confirm the goodness already there. (Holiness = reunited to the whole = goodness = what *is*.)

Job, essentially, just holds his ground. He threatens and curses the Lord, but there is already a freedom within him that the Lord recognizes from the beginning. He has identified the meaning of his life within himself, in terms of his relatedness to the Lord, rather than drawing it from without. His "ontological mooring," as Gabriel Marcel would call it, is in his union with God and not in his private or autonomous self-image.

In spiritual direction this is a crucial line that sooner or later a person has to cross, but some people never do. Some continue to draw their authority from without, to draw their name and identity from others, along with their happiness or sadness. René Girard speaks of this as "mimetic consciousness" (horizontal rivalry and desire and imitation), which always leads to catastrophe.

When people are named from within "by God," and the outer circumstances don't make a great deal of difference, then grace has triumphed within them. How am I defined? Are we defined by people's response to us each moment? If we are, we've built on a very subjective and sandy foundation. We'll be up and down constantly. Similarly, if we are defined by how good we're feeling or how successful we are, that, too, is a fragile definition of success. Here again, we will always be up and down. It is the shallowness of a secular/consumer culture as opposed to an authentic religious culture.

If how we feel each morning depends on whether people are nice to us, if we can't be happy without outside approval, we're not really happy or fundamentally free. Happiness is finally an inside job. We are too often "reeds swaying in the breeze" (Matt. 11:7), dependent moment by moment on others' reaction and approval. This is the modern self: insubstantial, whimsical, totally *dependent* and calling itself "free."

I have worked with people in whom I have seen the change. Once they were responding primarily to life outside themselves, but through contact with what I will call "authentic transcendence" they're drawing their life from within. They're not letting other people name them. They are named by God and they have recognized that name as their deepest and truest self. There is no this-world solution to the problem of ultimate identity and significance. Thus religion speaks of being saved from beyond, by God.

Without ontological grounding we can only *react* from womb to tomb. Life becomes an eternal hall of mirrors. We can never be stable in a life of reaction, because our significance is dependent on others or on our own cleverness and self-talk. "Salvation from God," by contrast, is a gift of self, from the one who is more truly me than I am by myself. Think about that — for the rest of your life perhaps.

It's not about sin

The Book of Job proclaims from the beginning that there is no correlation between sin and suffering, between virtue and reward. That logic is hard for us to break. This book tries to break it, so that a new logos, called grace, can happen.

Job's friends come in and counsel him. They are proper, believing religious people. And they offer all the typical solutions. Every stock phrase we've ever heard from clergy stereotypes, or read in pious books, is here. And they are rather intelligent, but the conclusion of the book is that none of these remedies is adequate or even correct.

They are all based on the same assumption: We're suffering, so we must have sinned. The three and eventually four friends of Job are intent on preserving their notion of God, their notion of Job, and their notion of justice at all costs. As I see it, they perfectly represent the most common masquerades for true biblical faith: ideology, orthodoxy, conventional wisdom, and heroic idealism. These all work to some degree until one comes up against the absurd, the ridiculous, the clearly unjust.

The difference between Job and his advisers is that they want and demand clarity and order from the universe. They want to foresee what God will do. Job wants to see God. They want to preserve a world of correct and coherent ideas. Job wants to preserve his relationship with God, even if it means his "littlement." His friends preserve their theologies. Job preserves his relationship. Job is the suffering-man-who-should-not-be-suffering and prefigures Jesus the dying-man-who-should-not-be-dying. Both of them bring us to the essence of what religious faith must mean. Both expand the possibility of human freedom to the edge — where only divine union can sustain us, where our life is not just about us.

The fairness factor

There is a term in moral theology called "retributive justice." We expect retribution of God and of one another: We do this or that good and expect this much back; we do this much bad and expect that much punishment. Our horribly expressed doctrine of purgatory was a perfect example of poorly understood retributive justice: We did so many things wrong, and we got ten years in the fire; we did some more things wrong and got fifteen years in the fire. As if fire were ever going to make things just or repay a debt to anybody.

The people who formulated this teaching were probably a lot like the four friends of Job, who saw life in terms of strict retributive justice. Conversely, if one enjoyed too much pleasure, one would have to make up for it with a certain amount of suffering. That thinking represents a superficial sense of equality that, nevertheless, most human beings carry around inside, namely, that everything has to balance out. Because we keep score, we assume God is Scorekeeper writ large.

This also assumes that God does not like pleasure and

gets some kind of cosmic justice out of burning people. How could that possibly reestablish truth? Untested faith tends to produce a very mechanistic and impersonal spirituality. Mature faith, however, almost always has a quality of paradox and mystery about it — as if to leave room for the freedom of God.

The underlying truth in the original folk belief in purgatory, for example, was that there is room for growth and life *after* death. Why should there not be more room for response after death? We don't have to make the moment we call human death the absolute finish line for human growth. Indeed, there seems to be some spiritual recognition in most people that we don't have to end the human story there. It is part of our belief in immortality, and probably finds its most urgent longing in the Book of Job. In some ways the story of Job is the ultimate climax and the final frustration of the Hebrew scriptures. It longs for a justice that we seldom achieve in this world and artificially creates it in the final chapter.

The Book of Job is very different from other books of the Old Testament for a number of reasons. It is in large part poetry and might well be described as drama in poetic form. It makes no pretense to being historical. It does not refer to the usual things other Old Testament books refer to: no Sinai, no covenant, law, liturgy, no reference to the exodus or the desert or any historical figures. It's obviously set apart from that whole Jewish history and made to stand on its own merits and its own foundations. Job is not even a Jew.

Whereas most of the Old Testament is preoccupied with corporate morality, with the people as a whole being good or bad, punished and rewarded, Job is concerned with one individual's moral dilemma. By the time Job appears we're getting late in the Old Testament period. This emerging individual morality — an individual in his private relationship with God — is a corrective and balance to the strong corporate morality of the earlier Old Testament.

Now, twenty-five hundred years later, we come from such an individualistic tradition that we have to be stretched the other way to understand corporate morality. The way Job thinks is akin to how we think today: that it's between me and God. So this book is an anomaly in the Old Testament, but it is very contemporary for Westerners and for both the secular and the religious mind.*

Will the real Job . . . ?

Is Job a historical character? It appears there existed an ancient legend of a pious man named Job. The legend probably matches the first chapter of this book as far as verse 21, and the last six verses in the book. Our anonymous author, five hundred years before Christ, took this old legend, perhaps an oral tradition, and expanded it to create a profound theology of the problem of evil, of conversion, growth, and suffering.

A good dramatist, the author brings in various characters to question the protagonist or hero, in order to get us involved in the drama. Job is symbol of the just Everyman, the good person, the person of faith.

"There was once a man in the Land of Uz called Job." (We don't know where Uz was, precisely; it might be fictional.) "A sound and honest man who feared God and shunned evil." There we have our Everyman with whom, it is hoped, we can all identify.

These early verses set it up in story form, like a fairy tale: "Seven sons and three daughters were born to him. And he owned seven thousand sheep, three thousand camels, five hundred yoke of oxen and five hundred she-donkeys, and many servants besides."

They simply set him before us in a straightforward way. But soon things begin to happen: "One day the sons of God came to attend on Yahweh." What does that mean? (In the New Testament we refer to Jesus as the Son of God. Notice how language emerges and changes: Later authors

---

*See William Safire, *The First Dissident* (Random House, 1992).

wouldn't use that language, as if to imply there were many sons of God.)

The Jews had the idea, at this stage of their development, of a whole council of holy people gathered around Yahweh. But, interestingly, among them was Satan. Later theology would never talk this way either. It is a fine example of the development of theology. Today, one would never think of Satan as one of the sons of God. Yet here he is, part of the council of heaven, advising God. Later thinkers such as Carl Jung were quite happy to find evil "integrated" into God in this story.

Satan deserves special mention. The word "Satan" is used only four times in the whole Old Testament. It's a Hebrew word which literally means "the accuser" or "the adversary." The one who is against. Yet the reason Satan is mentioned only four times, and only late in the Old Testament period, is because in much of the Old Testament God is seen as the cause of evil just as much as good. Only a developing of doctrine and philosophy of causality would lead us to make distinctions. Don't let anyone tell you that theology and belief have not evolved.

So who causes evil?

Later theology couldn't deal with this. More evolved theologians insisted God could only cause good. They needed someone else to blame evil on and named this totally bad and totally separate character Satan. There are many examples to show that this was no problem in the earlier period.

Amos 3:6, for example: "Shall there be evil in the city and the Lord has not done it?" Of course the Lord has done it was the insinuation, and at the time of Amos, eight centuries before Christ, they have no trouble saying so.

In Exodus we have Yahweh hardening the heart of the pharaoh. Here again, God does both good and bad things. This God of double standards persists even into the New

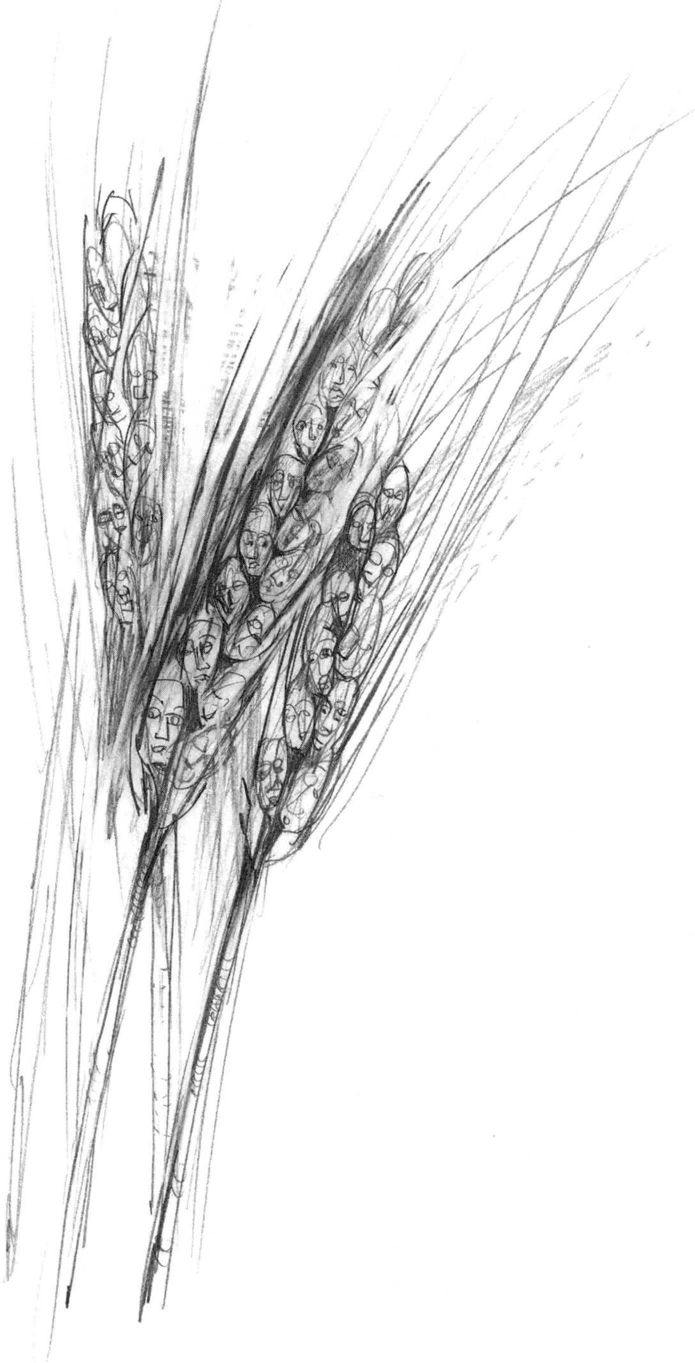

Testament period, until the time of Clement of Rome in the second century after Christ, who says, "God has a right hand and a left hand and both of them bring about his will." In other words, one brings good and the other evil. Modern theologians, as we know, have trouble with talk like that.

One physiological way to explain this is by reference to the two parts of our brain.

The right brain controls the left part of the body; the left brain controls the right part of our body. Science has only recently discovered that they both know reality in different ways. The right brain knows reality synthetically, holistically. It doesn't take things apart but rather puts things together. It looks less at text and more at context.

The left brain prefers analysis as a method of knowing reality. It analyzes each word, each part. Left-brain consciousness tends to create either-or thinking. If this is true, that can't be true. Logic calls these disjunctives. So Western Christianity creates dozens of denominations, for example. Each group thinks it possesses the only way to be saved, that it is the only group going to heaven. Left-brain and linear thinking can't deal with the reconciliation of opposites; it is impatient and even rejecting of paradox or mystery. That's the gift of the right brain, when it is aided by humility and grace.

One major reason the scriptures have been so distorted, and increasingly so in the last five hundred years, is because most European and North American minds have become so entirely left brain that they cannot deal with paradox. They can't deal with both-and. They impose their definitions of God on reality instead of letting reality reveal God. They can't accept a nuanced or veiled truth that isn't as neat as their words would like to make it.

What we need today are people who have a sense of order (left brain) but also a sense of creativity (right brain). And when those two aspects inform and respect each other, we have whole people. Most people in Western civilization are left-brain oriented. Right-brain-dominant people are too creative or too chaotic to fit in our system, as most of us would be too "rational" to fit into primal cultures.

Every time we walk, we're coordinating the right and left brain. Even little babies have to go through a crawling period and should not go straight from scooting to walking, because in the crawling period they're learning how to coordinate both halves of their brain.

We have learned how to move forward with motor skills, but we have not learned how to move forward with our spiritual or psychic skills. We need to listen to reality both ways.

We have to order reality. I could not write without left-brain skills. Nor could you read. But if it stops there, it goes nowhere. The left brain by itself is stunted. It's not creative. It isn't life-giving. It isn't the source of power. It doesn't have energy and it doesn't make connections. These are the function of the right brain.

Then there was Satan

The point of all this is that the Bible is much more right-brain literature than left-brain. The Hebrew people were not subject to the sophisticated civilization we have been subject to. They had no problem with paradox, with both-and. That's why they can bring Satan up into heaven and make him God's counselor. His advice wasn't very good, but he did advise. The name wasn't yet capitalized, it just meant "adversary." In the canonization process we have a special role for "the devil's advocate," the person who takes the other side in legal issues, who stands against. In the debate of life, it is always affliction and controversy that bring about a greater truth.

Yahweh at a certain stage says to Satan, "Where have you been?" And Satan responds, "Round the earth, roaming about" (1:8). This accuser, this adversary, in other words, is everywhere.

We might refer to him today as "the negative voices,"

although that is not an adequate definition of Satan. But it would denote one form of the demonic. The negative voices that assault people every day and tell them they are unacceptable, stupid, not good enough.

The great spiritual writers say it's unfortunate we have such a caricature of Satan — the man with a pitchfork and tail, almost funny. (It is interesting that no one complains about sexist images here!) This evil roaming the world is more likely in a sophisticated, gentlemanly disguise. Gallant, even. A well-dressed scholar, for example, not the kind most of us would dream of questioning. As Paul says, "the angels of darkness disguise themselves as angels of light" (2 Cor. 11:14). Any of us would readily reject Satan if he came up to us as a little guy with a red tail! The problem is his three-piece suit. And he is probably living the American dream, a nice guy who smiles, shakes your hand, has lovely children, does all the right things, maybe even going to church on Sunday. That's the only way he'll be believable.

It's amazing that it has taken us so long to unmask Satan. To recognize he is "roaming the earth." The principle of evil is everywhere in disguise and is even in the courts of the sons of God. It's so easy to be confused. In times of trial, in fear, Satan is going to look like the answer to our problems. We'll be inclined to say to his promptings, "Well, that's a reasonable suggestion."

Yahweh goes on, "Did you notice my servant, Job? There is no one like him on the earth: A sound and honest man who fears God and shuns evil."

Satan replies, "Yes, but Job is not God-fearing for nothing, is he? Have you not put a wall about him?" So let's test him, the wily Satan suggests. "Stretch out your hand and lay a finger on his possessions: I warrant you, he will curse you to your face." There we have the initial wager that sets the whole drama in motion. Can a human being love God "for nothing"?

"Very well," Yahweh says to Satan. "All he has is in your power." So he gives Satan permission to wreak havoc on Job, and the rest of the book waits to find who wins the bet — God or Satan.

Satan is not exactly commissioned by God, but he is at least given permission by God to do what he wants. Still, there are some restrictions: "Keep your hands off his person." So Satan takes his leave of Yahweh, unable to actually touch "the person" or essential self of Job.

Two words of Greek origin are important at this stage: "symbolic" and "diabolic."

Symbolic means to throw together. Diabolic means to throw apart. Evil is always dualistic, always separates: body from soul, heart from head, human from divine, masculine from feminine. Whenever we separate, evil comes into the world.

People I have known with psychotic or neurotic problems invariably have been emotionally divided. One part of their emotional life is affirmed, another part repressed — don't think that, don't feel that. Thus, one part of their humanity is denied. We all find myriad ways to divide, to separate: "You're not an acceptable person because of your color or religion or race." Whenever we divide, we destroy.

Symbolism, however, always reconnects what has been thrown apart. This probably explains why healthy religion ("re-ligio"=bind back together), throughout history, gives us symbols, images of reconciliation, that heal, that put together what has been taken apart. One pays a high price for reconciliation. God is always the great reconciler and healer of opposites — even sin and goodness. God holds together our person; Satan always tries to divide us.

The trials of being a bridge

During my sojourn with the peace movement in Germany, we were trying to provide the members with a foundation built on faith. Much of the movement was based on fear, anger, expedience, and an array of strange philosophies. A huge number of people were involved, and it was sad to see how few had come to their conclusions and commitments through faith or contact with true transcendence. In that regard the American peace movement has been much stronger than the European movement.

I found myself, after a few weeks, trying to be a bridge, getting people who never talked to each other to communicate. East and West each thought the other was a focus of evil, a blunder most famously expressed by President Reagan's "Evil Empire." As long as we presume the focus of evil is on the other side, there is no hope of reconciliation. Satan, the "accuser," is always projecting evil elsewhere and attacking it over there.

We all have some evil within ourselves. We all have the roots of violence within us. Until we take responsibility for that, we will continue to need victims and continue to create victims.

The word *pontifex* means bridge-builder. The word is applied preeminently to the Holy Father: *Pontifex Maximus* means the greatest bridge-builder. History hints that the pope has not always been that, but the word shows that's what the early church expected from the bishop of Rome.

I personally took great comfort from being a bridge-builder, connecting people who don't usually connect. I hoped new life would come out of that. But I learned after a while that you pay a price for being a bridge—people walk on you from both sides.

Both the right and the left, the capitalists and communists, however we describe the polarities, both sides use you for their own purposes. When you stand for the Gospel, you are in a very vulnerable position. Everybody thinks you're in it for ideology's sake. They want to put you in a box right away. Then inevitably you're seen to be in a box for the other side, and they hate you and presume you're wrong.

In East Germany, we tried to introduce ourselves with a bit of humor: "We are working for peace in our country, so we are constantly told that our salaries are paid by communist countries." They just laughed and laughed and said, "That's exactly what they tell us here — that we're getting paid by your U.S. government!"

The world is afraid of reconciliation. We prefer to live in a world of black and white where we create and maintain enemies, because that keeps our own group together.*

It has probably been this way since the beginning of time. Our human nature has trapped us in certain positions that have a degree of culture-forming logic to them but overall are simply untrue.

How can God change all that? I think the answer is in the Book of Job. God can set us right only by breaking us down. As long as we remain in a self-assured, righteous, left-brain position, there is no way we can be bridge-builders or reconcilers. We're going to see in Job how God breaks this man down so he can enter into a newer and better definition of truth, a better understanding of how God creates life on earth.

It seems that God's definition of goodness and order includes some evil. Evil and affliction seem to be a part of the plan and pattern by which we come to God. The Book of Job is a commentary on our struggle with this unwelcome pattern.

I don't believe God creates evil, yet God clearly allows it and even makes use of it. This is where words break down. But we can't deny that evil is roaming the earth, so it obviously came from somewhere. Is evil merely "the absence of good," as some philosophers have said? Or is evil a positive entity? This question is, of course, debated through the centuries.

But more importantly, what does God do about it? I think this will be the final revelation of God's greatness, that God somehow uses evil and suffering in our favor.

---

*See Gil Bailie, *Violence Unveiled* (Crossroad, 1995).

God's role in evil

God did not create evil, but God created a definition of good that seems to include evil. I think that's just being honest and realistic. It's not being theological — it merely states what is obviously the case. God is surely tolerating evil; and it appears that, beyond tolerating, God is even making use of it. Maybe that is the great work of transformation, "bringing life out of death, and calling into being what does not exist" (Rom. 4:17). It could be called the foundational image of God for the Hebrews in Genesis, in Exodus, in Deuteronomy, and for the Christians in both Paul and Jesus.

Yahweh in the Old Testament is the totality of opposition; everything comes from God, including good and evil. Thus, for the ancient Hebrews there was no problem of evil.

Not until their moral conscience developed further did the Hebrews begin to be uncomfortable with a God who, apparently indiscriminately, sent both good and evil upon humankind. The Book of Job marks the end of simple consciousness and the beginning of a new awareness. The two "theologies" are intermingled. Satan is in the court of God, but there is the beginning of a break with the notion of God as source of evil.

Developing consciousness is more concerned with precise cause and effect. A big question becomes: Who is responsible? Some languages — as in the Philippines — don't even have verbs to express who is responsible. They say, for example, the fire got lit. My wife got pregnant. No clear sense of responsibility, no allocation of cause.

We, on the other hand, want to know who is responsible for the good and evil. We should be aware that this was not a primary question for the people in our scriptures. Until Job. Then there begins to be a stronger sense of individual personhood. "I know I didn't do anything bad, and I'm not going to take the rap for it."

The story of Job also makes us aware that we have paid a heavy price for our process of individuation. The private self, cut off from sacred union, is very vulnerable, insecure, and prone to either immense guilt and shame or dangerous inflation and illusion. Job is in many ways the beginning of the modern sense of self. He lives the struggle and pays the price in both guilt and defiance. Who of us cannot identify with him? And his loneliness?

Chapter 3

An Eye-Opener on Prayer

A STRIKING FACT about the Book of Job is that God does not seem eager to appear as the hero. On the contrary, Yahweh is quite content to let Job emerge finally heroic. This divine modesty is true not only of this book but of all our history. When you have real authority, you do not have to prove it. When you are truly in charge, you don't have to go throwing your weight around.

In the Book of Job, therefore, God does not burst on the scene like Superman to solve the problem. Instead, Yahweh remains quietly on the edge, observing and trusting. When you know you're in charge, you can wait, because you know you have the power to bring things together. It is a lesson not only in ultimate authority but also in the patience and even the humility of God.

Sometimes people who don't know God well presume that God would use power the way they would use power: as a dominative force. They want a *deus ex machina,* a magician God who appears out of the wings to solve the problem. The paradox of the Book of Job is that Yahweh remains totally present in power, yet to all appearances does nothing. And for thirty-seven chapters God says nothing. It's our worst nightmare: a silent, hidden, and ineffective God.

With friends like Job's, who needs trouble?

Job's three friends, practical, righteous, and religious, appear as God's self-appointed messengers with what they are sure is God's answer. They offer the glib, pious platitudes of stereotypical clergymen. They're all theologically correct, yet entirely inadequate. (There's a message in there somewhere for both left and right.)

What they do, in effect, is try to take away the mystery. They try to solve the problem, whereas Yahweh says you cannot solve the problem; you can only live the mystery. The only response to God's faithfulness is to be faithful ourselves.

Theology does not provide the answer to this dilemma, only spirituality does. It's disappointing that we Christians have emphasized theology so much more than spirituality. We have emphasized catechism and religious education much more than prayer. But for the predicament we have here, there is no answer, only a prayer response, only the willingness to remain in communion, to hang in there, to keep talking.

We see in the dialogues of Eliphaz of Teman, Bildad of Shuah, and Zophar of Naamath that they constantly talk about God. They're good men and their answers are, to a great extent, correct. But the only one who talks *to* God is Job. Out of his intense pain and depression — he is on the edge of despair, if not actually in despair, throughout the entire book — Job breaks through to address God.

This is probably one of the greatest books on prayer that has ever been written. It breaks our stereotypes of prayer. Certainly, most of the things Job says to God are not what we Christians have been trained to say to God. The pretty words are mostly gone. There's no "beseech" and "vouchsafe" and "deign" and "thou," the stuff Christians love to put in their formal prayers. Instead he dares to confront God, the very thing we were trained never to do. In fact, we called it blasphemy.

Job tries yelling at God

He yells at God, accuses God of all kinds of things, speaks sarcastically, almost makes fun of God. "If this is a game you're playing, then you're not much of a God! I don't need you and I don't want you" — it's that kind of prayer that creates saints. You can't pray that way, with that authority, unless you know something, unless you are assured at a deep level of a profound relatedness between the two of you, unless you know you can venture into that arena where we say angels fear to tread.

The desired relationship may be easier to understand for those who have lived a long marriage. The partners are aware what they have said to one another in the past. They have proven by their lives that they love one another. Against such a background one can tell the other off. Let 'em have it. There are the past forty years to fall back on, earlier intimacies to rely upon. Our history together is our truth, undeniable; the events of a lifetime are there, they can't be withdrawn. That's what Job is relying on and never really doubts.

In the first altercation between Satan and Yahweh, Satan predicts Job will immediately curse God. Job, however, proves Satan wrong. He even praises God: "Yahweh gave, Yahweh has taken back, blessed be the name of Yahweh." In all this misfortune, Job committed no sin nor offered any insult to God (1:21–22).

So, "once again, the sons of god came to attend to Yahweh, and among them was Satan." Here again, Satan is among the court of heaven. And Yahweh said to Satan, "Where have you been?"

"Around the earth, roaming about."

"Did you notice my servant, Job?" Here God is almost gloating. "Did you notice Job did not curse me?" is the implied taunt. "There is no one like him on earth: a sound and honest man who fears God and shuns evil. His life continues blameless as ever; in vain you provoked me to ruin him" (2:1–4).

Satan, however, isn't a devil for nothing. He doesn't give up easily. If only he were allowed to test Job a little further, he suggests, specifically to touch his person, Satan is confident that Job would "curse you to your face."

"Very well," Yahweh says, "he is in your power. But spare his life." So Satan again left the presence of Yahweh.

"He struck Job down with malignant ulcers from the sole of his foot to the top of his head. Job took a piece of a pot to scrape himself and went and sat in the ashpit" (2:5–8). We hear of Satan no more in the entire book. He has done his work: dividing and accusing.

Job's wife comes into the picture at this point. If Job has lost all his children and possessions, so has his wife. Mrs. Job is hurting too. And she's not the image of patience he is. She says, "Do you now still mean to persist in your blamelessness?" She wants him to admit he made some mistake. She's caught up in the retributive justice syndrome which believes he must have done something wrong or this wouldn't be happening. She demands that he admit it. "Curse God, and die" (2:9).

This is an interesting demand. She sees him at the edge of death and says, in effect, "At least get it out of your system, get it over with and die so I can get on with my life." But Job replies ideally, although still in shocked denial: "That is how foolish women talk. If we take happiness from God's hand, must we not take sorrow, too?" (2:10).

Here is the beginning of what we call the paschal mystery. All of life is a mixture of joy and sorrow, and we must accept both together. (But one is *not* a punishment or reward for the other. This is crucial.) In the mystery of Christ's death and resurrection, this becomes very dramatized, personalized, and correctly imaged. Both come together and we can't have one without the other. There has been a great temptation in many modern religious movements — like some in the charismatic movement or the "gospel of success" — to have the resurrection without the cross, to enjoy part of the mystery and to avoid the pain that *necessarily* goes with it.

On the other side, many moralistic, stoic, or Jansenistic types suffer their crosses diligently but refuse to recognize or enjoy Christ already risen in all things.

Worthwhile joy has pain stain

True joy is not authentic unless achieved *through* pain — not under it, not to the right or left or over, but through it. That's the only authentic Christian joy. Any other joy is a covering up of pain, an escaping and denying. There is much denial in religion. The old ostrich maneuver — pretend it's not happening. That's not what the Lord is calling us to; it's not the whole paschal mystery. It's not the mystery to which Job is submitting here. "If we take happiness from God's hand, must we not take sorrow, too? And in all his misfortune, Job uttered no sinful word" (2:10). So, again, he proves Satan wrong.

News of Job's disasters came to the ears of three of his friends. They are good friends. Each sets out from home. Their hometowns are all in an area called Edom, which is known for its gurus — like Nepal, for example.

By common consent the gurus go to offer him consolation. Seeing him from a distance, they cannot recognize him. Their concern for him is genuine. They weep. They tear their garments, throw dust over their heads, and sit on the ground beside him for seven days and seven nights. Faithful friends. If someone is near death or has just lost a loved one, there's not a great deal to say. All words fall short. Often, all we can offer is our presence, just being there. But strength is communicated, caring is communicated.

We may experience this especially at a wake. We may sit there, maybe for hours, knowing no words are adequate. Especially if the grief has some tragic or nonsensical character. Job has such friends. They never say a word, so sad a sight he makes.

At the heart of the Book of Job are the famous dialogues

(chapters 3–31), rendered in poetic form, often described as perhaps the most perfect religious poem ever written. It may also be the oldest Hebrew poem to have survived.

After sitting there for seven days, in the end it is Job who breaks the silence. The others have not dared to say anything — they are reeling with the mystery of it all. So Job speaks up and curses like this: "May the day perish when I was born and the night that told of a boy conceived." He lambastes both the day of his birth and the day of his conception — he's in a hell of a rage.

Job's stages of dying

This whole section foreshadows Elisabeth Kübler-Ross's well-known stages of grief and dying: denial, anger, bargaining, resignation, and acceptance. The first seven days of silence and the immediate perfect response match the first stage — denial. But now we reach the anger stage. Pages and pages of anger and cursing. He is saying, in effect, "This so-called life I have is not really life, God, it is death. So why should I be happy about being born?"

Some years ago, I sat with a woman in Detroit who had experienced suffering like Job's. She and her husband were spending their lives trying to build community in the inner city. They moved into a difficult area, lived there for ten years, had little of what we might call success. Yet they remained faithful — and they would not have been able to fake it in that situation.

Then, their youngest daughter was raped. We sat on her front porch and the mother talked something like this: "I cannot believe that death would be worse than what I'm experiencing right now. I wake up every day and I want to die. I feel used, abused, not respected by God. I risked everything for God and this is what I get. No way can I describe the anger, the absolute rage I feel at every level of my being. And no matter how long I live, I can't imagine there's going to be another day that I'm not going to think of this. Why should my life have to be this way? I have one life. People generally look forward to living their later years in some kind of peace, but I'm going to have to live with this. And I just don't know whether I can do it." I was stunned by the truth and pain of her words.

Not being that mother, not having a daughter of my own, I could only partially identify with what she was feeling. Yet, such experiences perhaps help us to understand what this author is trying to communicate through the mouth of Job.

"May that day be darkness. May God on high have no thought for it, may no light shine on it. May murk and deep shadow claim it for their own" (3:4). It's beautiful, poetic imagery. He's saying: Uncreate that day. Make it not a day of light, but darkness. Let clouds hang over it, eclipse swoop down on it. Where God in Genesis says, "Let there be light," Job now says, "Let there be darkness." The day of uncreation, of anticreation. You probably have to have experienced true depression or betrayal to understand such a feeling.

There's a part of each of us that feels and speaks that sadness. Not every day, thank goodness. If we're willing to feel and participate in the pain of the world, part of us will suffer that kind of despair. If we want to walk with Job and in solidarity with much of the world, we must allow grace to lead us there as the events of life show themselves. I believe this is exactly what we mean by conformity to Christ.

We must go through the stages of feeling, not only the last death but all the earlier little deaths. If we abort these emotional stages by easy answers, all they do is take a deeper form of disguise and come out in another way. So many people learn that the hard way — by getting ulcers, by all kinds of internal diseases, depression, irritability, and misdirected anger — because they refuse to let their emotions run their course or to find some appropriate place to share them.

It's obvious Job is not an Anglo-Saxon. He's not afraid to

feel his feelings. He acts and speaks them out. So Job may have all kinds of ulcers on the outside, but he's not likely to get them on the inside, as we tend to do.

Emotions ought to be allowed to run their course. Emotions are not right or wrong; they have no moral meaning. One does not go to confession to confess having emotions, no matter how negative they are. They are merely indicators of what is happening.

People who do not feel deeply finally do not *know* deeply either. Because Job is willing to feel his emotions, he is able to come to grips with the mystery in his head and heart and gut — he understands holistically.

Let there be darkness, he says. "Let that night be dismal, no shout of joy come near it. Let them curse it who curse the day.... Dark be the stars of its morning, let it wait in vain for light and never see the eyelashes of dawn" (3:7–9). If you can't feel it from the text, this is the appropriate emotion of rage — and directed to the whole universe!

Job feels the heat

Then Job moves into the bargaining stage. Why? he asks. Questioning is often the beginning of bargaining. "Why did I not die newborn, not perish as I left the womb? Why were there two knees to receive me [his father], two breasts for me to suck [his mother]?" (3:11–12).

Next he describes Sheol. The closest Christian equivalent to Sheol is Limbo. Even here in the late Old Testament, they have not yet developed much of a theology of eternal life, our understanding of which comes primarily from the teaching of Jesus. We can see the implications in this book. If there were a belief in life after death, Job would not have such a difficult time. He could console himself as Christians do: He could put up with all this and there would be a revelation of significance later.

But this life is all Job has, which is still the belief of many

Jewish people. As a result, many Jews take this world much more seriously than many Christians do. They often tend to involve themselves in correcting social injustices more than Christians and are not afraid of beauty, sex, and dancing. "This is all we have; we have to make it into a good world. We have to be involved in it. When we die, it's over. This is it."

For the purification of our faith, it is important first to be "Jews in spirit," to have that kind of faith. The life of virtue and God-centeredness is an end in itself, and not for the sake of some future reward. To do what God wants simply because God is God. That's what Job is dealing with. What a profound faith that many Christians have never even considered. Pius X was truly magisterial when he said that Catholics needed to be "spiritually Semites."

Forget heaven and hell. Pretend that the day we die, that's it. How many of us would bother to study scripture at all? How many would bother even to be good? Our training in the reality of heaven and hell has influenced our entire way of thinking, and not always for the good.

No one can take the consolation and gift of immortality away from us, yet such promises have also made Christian people rather sloppy in our thinking and faith. It has allowed us not to take history seriously. It has allowed us to be, as it were, absentee landlords in this world, to just muddle through, to make sure we go to church on Sunday so we get the reward later — or avoid some punishment. Fire insurance is not happy or healthy religion.

Pure Jewish faith is for the sake of faith itself. Faith that God is God and I am a creature. God is good and I am to be like God. But not for the sake of a later reward.

These considerations are essential for understanding this book. Job draws his satisfaction from truth and justice, not from hope of future reward or fear of future punishment.

This concept of Sheol was the most the Jewish people anticipated. Maybe it wasn't eternal life, but a place of dust and darkness where there's some kind of quasi-existence.

There's not much satisfaction in Sheol, but there is no punishment either. It is nonworld, a picturesque denial of all that we know here. The Greeks had a similar thing they called Hades. It was a lazy theology that eventually developed those ancient concepts into what Christians think of as hell, a place of torture. The New Testament *metaphor* of Gehenna, the garbage dump of Jerusalem, "where the worm never dies and the fire never goes out" (Isa. 66:24) didn't help us much either. For some self-loathing reason we tend to take negative metaphors literally and dismiss positive metaphors — such as "your names are written in heaven" (Luke 10:20) — as innocuous poetry.

The torture aspect emerged precisely from the three friends' *misunderstanding* of retributive justice: that the only way God is going to make things right is by vengeful punishing. There is no way that the scriptures reveal a God who is an eternal torturer. Yet many Christians seem to believe this, and many are even held back from trusting God's goodness because of this "angry parent in the sky" that we have created. Such teachers, like Job's, are false friends of God and of humanity. The general belief of the scriptures, however, is that God's justice is not achieved by punishment, but by the divine initiative we call grace, which enables us to bring about internal rightness, harmony, balance, and realignment with *what is:* God.

In other words, God "justifies" (read "validates") creation not by parental punishment from without, but by positive enticement and transformation from within. Surely a far greater victory and achievement of "justice" on God's part. This concept of grace is first called mercy, *hesed,* the ever faithful, covenant-bound love of God. I would go so far as to call it *the primary revelation* of the entire Bible. If you miss this message, all the rest is distorted and even destructive. I cannot emphasize this strongly enough.

The problem of not being God

Our most basic theological problem is that God is God and we're not. Most of us in effect are terribly upset that we're not God. It really ticks us off that another is in charge and we're not, and that we're only creatures. We spend much of our life railing and complaining because we're not in charge and we can't call the shots — at least I do.

Job, too, is upset that he is not God. Yet he never carries that rebellion all the way. He finally submits, and occasionally even breaks into a kind of revelry, delighting in God being God. At such times he seems rather glad that he's not in charge, which is a wise response for a human.

In verse 3:20 he moves back into his questioning mode. Now he questions God's goodness and judgment: "Why give light to a man of grief? Why give life to those bitter of heart, who long for a death that never comes, and hunt for it more than for a buried treasure? They would be glad to see the grave mound and shout with joy if they reached the tomb. Why make this gift of light to a man who does not see his way, whom God balks on every side?" Sounds like the midlife crisis when we say in one form or another, "What is it all for?"

In verses 3:24–26 he moves into what can only be called self-pity: "My only food is sighs. My groans pour out like water." Have you ever exhaled all day, as if to regurgitate the sad taste of life? Job's sadness is the opposite of eating: emptying out, with nothing to take in and nothing to satisfy.

"Whatever I fear comes true, whatever I dread befalls me," Job goes on with his own version of Murphy's Law. The worst thing that can happen, happens. "For me there is no calm, no peace, my torments banish rest." On this whimpering note Job rests his case.

"Good" advice

Now the first of the advisers comes forward, Eliphaz of Teman, the oldest and most gentlemanly of the three. He appeals to his own personal religious experience.

All three of them, we eventually find, try to give appropriate answers, the answers they learned in catechism class. The responses of Eliphaz might be described as worldviews that harden into ideology. They emphasize a certain perspective to the neglect of others, as ideology always does. Today we sometimes speak of such people as "agenda-driven." Ideology is a very common masquerade for real faith because the agenda looks so good or religious. This is similar to efficient church operations masquerading as loyalty to God.

"If one should address a word to you," Eliphaz begins, "will you endure it?" Are you going to open up? as we might say today. "Yet who can keep silent?" Surely not me, thinks Eliphaz! "Many another, once, you schooled, giving strength to feeble hands; your words set right whoever wavered, and strengthened every failing knee. And now your turn has come, and you lose patience too; now it touches you, and you are overwhelmed" (4:1–5).

Eliphaz is saying, "I'm going to be the teacher now for a change, and you're going to be the student, and look how impatient you already are."

"Does not your piety give you confidence," he goes on, "your blameless life not give you hope?"

This smacks of sarcasm — maybe Job is not so blameless after all, because who can recall a guiltless man ever perishing, as Job looks likely to do at any moment? Job ought to know there's a strict law of retribution, according to Eliphaz. In our day we might self-righteously tell Job he needs to go to confession. The harsh, all-too-human conclusion is: "You're brought to nothing, Job, so you can't be such a good man." It's called blaming the victim.

We can't always give those easy answers. We generally want to rush enthusiastically in and speak blithely of God's will: "Well, there must be a reason for it." The newly converted and the newly ordained response that wants order at all costs, even if truth or compassion must be sacrificed.

Even God not always in charge

But when Jesus sat looking down on Jerusalem and crying over it, the last thing he needed was a pious soul to run up to him and say, "Now, Jesus, don't cry. It's all in God's perfect plan. In fact, it's even prophesied in the scriptures."

No. Let Jesus cry. Crying is a different mode entirely than fixing, explaining, or controlling. We need to cry more, I think. How's that for Franciscan spirituality!

We have the mistaken idea that God is totally in charge. But in John's letter and Gospel Jesus says very clearly that Satan is prince of this world (1 John 5:19; John 12:31).

God is very seldom in charge, it seems to me. Only in the lives of saints, only in people who know themselves and love the Lord and one another is God possibly in charge. In the rest of us, God is in charge maybe a few moments a day.

Remember that the opposite of love is not really hatred, but *control.* God remains in love and therefore out of the control mode. When we are not in love, we are invariably trying to control everything — it's a good litmus test. God seems to be fully in control only when *we* give it back to God. That is the beauty and limitation of those who love. They can give up control, and they can weep instead of explain.

Anecdotal theology

In verse 4:8, Eliphaz says, "I speak of what I know." Notice how he is too easily relying on his own experience and universalizing from it.

He goes on to describe his personal religious experience:

"Now, I have had a secret revelation, a whisper has come to my ears." It sounds like some of your friends saying, "God told me."

"At the hour when dreams master the mind [he even shrouds it in mystery—it came in the middle of the night], and slumber lies heavy on man, a shiver of horror ran through me [now it's becoming dramatic, you can practically hear the organ music in the background], and my bones quaked with fear. A breath slid over my face, the hairs of my body bristled. Someone stood there—I could not see his face, but the form remained before me. Silence—and then I heard a voice, 'Was ever any man found blameless in the presence of God, or faultless in the presence of his maker? In his own servants God puts no trust, and even with his angels he has fault to find. What, then, of those who live in houses of clay, who are founded on dust?" (4:13–19).

The entire effect is to give transcendent weight to what is, after all, only his own opinion. I have done it more than once myself, but it doesn't work in the end.

What then of you? is the gist of Eliphaz. If God finds fault with the angels, who are you, Job? "They are crushed as easily as a moth.... Their tent peg is snatched from them, and they die for lack of wisdom." (There is heavy irony in that line. He is accusing Job of lack of wisdom, whereas it is clearly Eliphaz himself who lacks anything beyond conventional wisdom.)

Now, don't get mad, Job!

"Make your appeal, then," Eliphaz continues to taunt Job. "Will you find an answer? To which of the holy ones will you turn? Resentment kills the senseless [he's telling Job not to feel his feelings], and anger brings death to the fool." It is ironic that Eliphaz appeals to his experience to tell Job not to trust his own: a common ploy of religious folk engaging in moral one-upmanship.

We also think that if people don't get angry, the problem will go away. But this isn't necessarily so. And there's nothing inherently wrong with anger. Don't tell them to take away their anger: It's only by working through it and understanding their anger and owning their anger that people understand what's going on. We need to exercise our emotions and should not listen to Eliphaz's advice about anger.

(Yet he is right about "resentment killing." Resentment usually refers to states of long-term anger that only blind and deaden the one who resents. Thus Paul teaches wisely, "Never let the sun set on your anger or you will give the devil a foothold" [Eph. 4:27]. When we wrap ourselves around our anger, it possesses us like a demon.)

In verse 17, Eliphaz slips into a kind of easy optimism laced with encouragement: "Happy indeed the man whom God corrects." Not exactly what we want to hear when we're really hurting. Even patient Job probably felt like punching him.

"Do not refuse this lesson from Shaddai," Eliphaz goes on. Yahweh is sometimes referred to as El Shaddai — the God of the mountains. It is thought by some to be translated "the breasted one" and might be used as a nurturing and feminine image for God. This was a very ancient name, probably going back to the Jews' primitive, even preexodus experience. Eliphaz is trying to sound very traditional and orthodox.

"For he who wounds is he who soothes the sore, and the hand that hurts is the hand that heals." Sounds like one of those inspirational greeting cards. "Six times he will deliver you from sorrow, and the seventh, evil shall not touch you" (5:18–19). He is right, of course, but still utterly wrong.

So he makes Job all kinds of promises and assures him of multiple blessings. They are, not surprisingly, material blessings: "You shall laugh at drought and frost, and have no fear of the beasts of the earth.... You shall find your tent secure...you shall see your descendants multiply" (5:22, 24–25).

He's promising him, as it were, all these Cadillacs. What he's appealing to is the acquisitive or profit motive. A striking contrast to this can be found all the way through: All Job ever asks for is death. He never asks to get his money or possessions back, although this is what people are always offering him. They are coming from a basic materialist worldview. For all Job's despair, he is not a materialist — he never asks to get anything back. On the contrary, his thrust is: "I don't care for all that stuff. I want inner truth, and if I can't have that, I want death."

But these people who surround Job are dangerous because they are materialists who think they are spiritual. A very toxic and very common combination today. Talk about a good disguise! Even from the self.

The case is airtight, as Eliphaz sees it; no way Job can resist it. We will learn later that Job does not buy it. Job's questions remain unanswered. He responds, in effect: "You don't understand. You're not feeling my feelings. You're on a head trip, Eliphaz, and I know it's supposedly correct, but it isn't helping me a bit." It's hard to protect oneself from bad teaching when it is presented with sincerity, good intentions, and a certain degree of believability. Thus our frequent dilemma with fundamentalists and Catholic restorationists.

Lord, save us from Job's friends

As the story progresses, Job's erstwhile friends are perceived more and more as his enemies. Even though they may subjectively think they care for him, objectively they're at odds. This is a very important distinction because that's often the case in our own lives: People who like us, or mean us well, may be giving us poor advice, encouraging us to compromise, diverting us from our destiny. This is why we sometimes have to part even with our friends.

"If only my misery could be weighed," Job says, "and all

my ills be put on the scales. But they outweigh the sands of the seas. What wonder, then, if my words are wild?" (6:1–3).

Here he declares himself, as it were, in a position counter to that of Abraham. Abraham's children were to be as numerous as the sands by the sea, but for Job it is his suffering that multiplies like sand.

"The arrows of Shaddai stick fast in me, my spirit absorbs their poison, God's terrors stand against me in array" (6:4). Behind the bloated language in this section, what Job is saying is, "I'm hurting, guys, can't you feel anything for me? I don't need answers." From here on we will hear Job asking for some "redemptive listening" — from his friends and from God. In the spiritual life it's much more important to know how to listen than to know how to talk.

Most of us are not trained in redemptive listening. We're trained to give answers. In the counseling context, this listening mode is often called nondirective counseling. It is based on the premise that one can't ultimately provide the answers for others. All one can do is walk with the other and help others rightly to hear themselves. What people long to have happen is to be somehow received, understood. When they are heard, it seems, they can begin to hear. The most redemptive thing one can do for another is just to understand.

No one but God can capture the full projection of one's soul. When we're young, we try to fall in love with the perfect person who will totally understand us, and the great disappointment is to discover that no one person can.

That's what Job is asking, almost demanding: Someone, try to understand me. When we are understood, when we feel another person really cares, it's surprising how the problem, for the most part, can fade. We don't need the answer any more. The mere fact that someone is carrying the burden with us, walking with us on the journey, for some unbelievable reason — it's not logical at all — takes care of much of the problem.

That's the primary character of a true counselor, one who

can receive another's story. This is what Job asks for in his friends, and what humanity asks for in us: to skip the urge to give people answers, or to fix their problems. It seems all we can genuinely do is to *be there with life*. It's the only way we can overcome death. It's true friendship.

Chapter 4

Job and Friends Joust for God

WHEN HIS SO-CALLED FRIEND AND COUNSELOR Eliphaz finally stops talking, Job gets a chance to respond. In chapter 6 it's easy to see he's hurting and longing for someone to understand him.

"The very dishes which I cannot stomach, these are my diet in my sickness. Oh may my prayer find fulfillment, may God grant me my hope" (6:7–8). Here and elsewhere, Job's responses move back and forth between description, defense against his would-be friends, and, occasionally, beautiful prayers like this, which seem to arise from the pain. Sometimes the prayers are designed to protect himself against God, sometimes even to attack God. But he is still trying to trust God, to discover the foundation of hope.

He discovers that he hopes in spite of himself. There is no logic to this hope. It is "beyond reason." In the New Testament it will be called a gift of the Spirit, the gift of an uncreated hope (1 Cor. 13:13). Eventually we called faith, hope, and charity the "theological virtues" because they were a participation in the very life of God (who God is) as compared to other virtues which were practiced, imitated, and developed qualities. Hope here is "uncreated" because it's a communion with the one who is hope instead of the human creation of hopeful circumstances. These are two different realities, as every believer eventually discovers.

But his communion is not constant and he prays again for a kind of death: "May it please God to crush me, to give his hand free play and do away with me. This thought, as least, would give me comfort (a thrill of joy in unrelenting pain), that I had not denied the Holy One's decrees" (6:9–10). He does not lose his reverence for and trust in God, even though he is struggling to believe and praying for death.

Just so I know you are listening

The only thing that could now give Job satisfaction would be the knowledge that he's not estranged from God. If he could be assured that they are still in union, he could put up with whatever else God asks of him. This is why Job becomes the Old Testament symbol of ultimate faith: because all he is asking for is honest union — not success, not reward.

"But have I the strength to go on waiting?" he says. He's not sure he can persist in that kind of faith. "Has not all help deserted me?" These guys certainly are not any help, he ruminates. And in 6:15 he goes on, "My brothers have been fickle as a torrent, as the course of a seasonal stream."

Israel has streams that one can never depend upon. They may flood for weeks on end and then go for five years without a drop of water. His friends, he is now finding, are equally unreliable. What he needs them to say, they do not say; when he needs them to understand, they do not understand.

"Ice is the food of their dark waters, they swell with the thawing of the snow; but in the hot season they dry up.... Their trust proves vain." Or, as we say today, with friends like these, who needs enemies?

In 6:21 he says, in short, that he's not asking for much. "Have I said to you, 'Give me this or that, bribe someone for me at your own cost, snatch me from the clutches of an enemy or ransom me from a tyrant's hand'?" He wants them to sympathize with what he's going through instead of giving him theological answers. "Fair comment can be borne without resentment, but what is the basis for your strictures?" They're not being fair, he scolds them. Let them just show, if they can, where he has been at fault or how God is being just. He doesn't feel that is asking too much.

He makes no apology for complaining about God: "Do you think mere words deserve censure, desperate speech that the wind blows away?...Come, I beg you, look at me: As man to man, I will not lie. Relent and grant me justice; relent, my case is not yet tried" (6:26, 29).

Let's talk honestly person to person, "man to man." The text seems to be simultaneously talking to his friends and to Yahweh. He's begging them to treat him in a fair way. When you are overcome by self-doubt and self-criticism, the tiniest bit of understanding feels like a full body massage. Poor Job is begging for one.

Suffering is no fun, just ask Job

In chapter 7 he embarks on his extraordinary "soliloquy to suffering." Anyone hurting could open to this and be able to relate to many of its verses. "Is not man's life on earth nothing more than pressed service [those who have been in boot camp can probably understand], his time no better than hired drudgery? Like the slave sighing for the shade, or the workman with no thought but his wages, months of delusion I have assigned to me." He picks the three most miserable human conditions he can imagine: a slave, a hired hand, or a man in the military.

"Nothing for my own but nights of grief. Lying in bed I wonder when it will be day. Risen, I think how slowly evening comes. Restlessly I fret till twilight falls. Vermin cover my flesh, and loathsome scabs; my skin is cracked and oozes pus. Swifter than a weaver's shuttle my days have passed, and vanished, leaving no hope behind. Remember that my life is but a breath, and that my eyes will never again see joy" (7:1–6). Today, we would describe this as clinical depression and be watching for signs of suicide.

This author has a great awareness of the eyes. He waits to be *looked upon* lovingly by his friends and by God. The great triumph of the book is when he can finally believe, "God looks upon me and understands." The eyes are, as Jesus later says in the New Testament, the windows of the soul. We wait for an eye that looks through us and understands, an eye that receives us. Conversely, in verse 7 he laments, "My eyes will never again see joy." He longs to see joy. He waits for the "eye of blessing" from God — "the eye that once saw me will look on me no more, your eyes will turn my way, and I shall not be there" (6:8). That would be death.

Here begins what many consider a favorite part of the Book of Job. What emerges in several places is that Job still knows God likes him. Not loves him, but likes him. It's much harder for most people to believe that others like them than to believe others love them. It is even harder to believe that God could like us, not just our person but even our personality. Theoretically, theologically, we can accept that God loves us, but it's harder to believe that God could get excited about our company. When we can believe that, we're in the home stretch and feeling good about ourselves.

Job believes that! If God doesn't hurry up and solve this problem, he is saying, he won't be able to see Job any more: "Your eyes will turn my way and I will not be there." This reminds me of how my mother says I threatened her as a little boy: "If you don't wait on me, I might die and you won't have me anymore!" It was the strategy of a little tyrant. Yet it presumed an extraordinary love.

Here again is this belief in the finality of death that recurs throughout the book. When death comes, it's over, so hurry up, God, you don't have much time. Come on, I can't believe you don't want to see me. So take care of me or down I go into the pit never to be with you again. "As a cloud dissolves and is gone, so those who go down to Sheol never ascend again. He never comes home again, and his house knows him no more" (7:9–10).

Then he offers a most revealing prayer. Feeling the pain and separation, he cries out for communion with the Lord (verses 17–21).

Verse 17 is a contrast with Psalm 8, which asked: "What is man that you should notice him?" He's a little less than the angels, the psalmist answered his own question. And now Job asks: "What is man that you should make so much of him, subjecting him to your scrutiny, that morning after morning you should examine him, and at every instant test him?"

Not another happy prayer of praise and exultation, not a doxology, this is a profound prayer of betrayal and disappointment. Anyone who has lost a friend, or been abandoned, or rejected in love, can probably understand the depths such a prayer might come from.

Job had experienced similar closeness to God, and now, bereft of this communion, he simply cannot understand. He seems to be lashing out at God, but if we read between the lines we find he still loves God deeply. He's like the rejected spouse saying mean things to his or her partner when the real meaning is clear: "Dammit, you love me and I know you love me."

Similarly, between the lines we can see Job knows God loves him. "You can't mean this, God," is his gripe: "Will you never take your eyes off me long enough for me to swallow my spittle? Suppose I have sinned? What have I done to you, you tireless watcher of humankind? Why do you choose me as your target? Why should I be a burden to you? Can you not tolerate my sin, nor overlook my fault?"

In other words, if God is so great, why is Job's little sin troubling him so much? Can't God overlook Job's trifling faults? Job's parting shot is trying to both shame and invite God: "It will not be long before I lie in earth. Then you will look for me, but I will be no more." There's enormous trust there. He's now like a lost child afraid of being forgotten and ignored by one who surely loves him.

Happy they who can trust

I mentioned earlier that I used to manipulate my mother for attention. Apparently I loved milk and couldn't get enough of it. One hot summer day, I was repeatedly asking for milk, without success, so finally I put my hands on my hips, looked up at her and said, "Soon I'm going to be dead and you're not going to be able to get me milk ever again." She rushed to the refrigerator and got me the milk.

I couldn't have said something like that unless I totally trusted her love for me. And, like any child, I never imagined it wasn't her total delight to run to the refrigerator and get me another glass of milk twenty times a day. It never occurred to any of us that our mothers did not love doing all those things for us. We thought we were their whole life, never thought they might get tired or have other things to do.

Job, too, seems to rest "like a child in its mother's arms, like a weaned child in its mother's lap" (Ps. 131:2). Union, "ontological grounding" in God, is Job's only consolation.

Orthodox adviser

In chapter 8 the second adviser, Bildad the Shuhite, speaks up. This guy appeals to tradition, law, and God. He wants Job to admit he's wrong. He is also a spiritual materialist: He argues that if Job admits he is wrong, he'll get back everything he has lost.

Bildad is upset that Job is complaining against God and reprimands him for daring to question the Lord: "Is there no end to these words of yours, to your long-winded blustering? Can God deflect the course of right?" (8:1–2).

None of the three friends ever question their assumptions. They are smug in their theology. This guy has the whole truth — symbolizing the way most immature religious people tend to be: "I know the truth; don't bother me with the facts." Many of us live that way. We get our "truth" early in life and don't want to be bothered with further evidence.

"If your sons sinned against him, they have paid for their sins," Bildad forges ahead mercilessly. In other words, your kids are already dead. Shouldn't you realize you did something wrong? "Without delay he will restore his favor to you.... Your former state will seem to you as nothing beside your new prosperity" (8:4, 6–7). Prosperity, ironically, is precisely what Job is not asking for, but that's the world his friends are caught up in.

"Question the generation that has passed. Meditate on the experience of its fathers." This is the tradition, in other words. "We sons of yesterday know nothing; our life on earth passes like a shadow. But they will teach you, they will tell you, and these are the words they will speak from the heart" (8:8–10).

When we do something wrong, we will be punished—this is the alleged teaching. He expounds a version of natural law. "Without water, can the rushes grow?" Just as certain as those natural laws, when a man sins he is punished, when he is good he is rewarded. Makes sense. It just isn't what the saints say about God.

This "theology" is designed, basically, to compel us to save ourselves. Which is, unfortunately, what most people believe to this day — that we are going to get back as much as we give to God. This theory finally makes salvation depend upon us and our perfection and goodness.

It would be much truer to say we are brought to God by our weakness and brokenness—exactly the opposite of what most people think. It takes most of our lifetimes, even with grace, to accept such a paradox. Grace seems to create the very emptiness that grace alone can fill. "For it is in weakness that power reaches perfection... it is when I am weak that I am strong" (2 Cor. 12:9–10).

But Bildad goes on, in verse 8:20, to describe what seems like an irrefutable law: "Believe me, God neither spurns a stainless man, nor lends his aid to the evil. Once again your cheeks will fill with laughter, from your lips will break a cry of joy." Just get with the program, Job, and you will be back in the game.

One can see a touch of sarcasm in this verse, because Job could well be saying to himself, "Yes, things will get better, but not by following your advice." One does not discover true joy by compromising one's integrity — even with godly advice.

Faith isn't having answers

In chapter 9 Job tries to answer this second opponent, saying in effect, okay, you guys can praise God and affirm his greatness, but I can do it better than you. You've got nothing on me when it comes to teaching about the power of God.

"I know it is as you say," he tells them. "How can man be in the right against God?...His heart is wise, and his strength is great. Who then can successfully defy him?" (9:1, 4).

I know I don't have a chance, Job is saying, I know God is right somehow; I just don't understand in this instance how he's right. But I'm willing to wait.

That's the difference. He's willing to wait in that space of nonanswer. That's the space in which God creates faith. The counselors are not willing to live in that space where there is no answer, no conclusions. To this day, many people equate "religious answers" with "faith." But faith does not mean having answers; it means being willing to live without answers. Cultural faith and civil religion tend to define faith poorly and narrowly as having certitudes and being able to hold religious formulas.

Such common religion is often an excuse for *not* having faith. Strange, isn't it? *Faith is having the security to be insecure,* the security to live in another identity than our own and to find our value and significance in that larger union. Paul has achieved a much more precise articulation of this after Christ: "I live now not with my own life, but with the life of Christ who lives in me" (Gal. 2:20). It's almost like an identity transplant, switching to a larger fuel tank, and letting go of a smaller self that begs for supremacy. *And it always feels like dying.*

Every movement toward union will be experienced as a loss of self-importance and a loss of control. No wonder that faith is so rare and we substitute it with nice religion.

Job never diminishes God: "He moves the mountains, though they do not know it; he throws them down when he is angry. He shakes the earth, and moves it from its place, making all its pillars tremble. The sun at his command forbears to rise, and on the stars he sets a seal" (9:5–7).

So Job is pouring more lavish praise on God's power than his friends ever did. "He and no other stretched out the skies, and trampled the seas' tall waves.... His works are great, beyond all reckoning, his marvels past all counting. Were he to pass me, I should not see him, nor detect his stealthy movement. Were he to snatch a prize, who could prevent him, or dare to say, 'What are you doing?' "

I know God is God, in other words. I know God is in charge. I'm not doubting God's power or freedom. How dare I plead my cause, then? How dare I choose arguments against him? I know he makes the rules; it's just that I don't understand the rules he's making right now.

"Suppose I am in the right, what use is my defense? For he whom I must sue is judge as well" (9:15). Job sees it as a court case, one in which he does not have a chance. God, the one he is trying to sue, is also the judge. And he's God, while Job is no big deal.

In court, furthermore, "could I be sure that he would listen to my voice?" (9:16). Again notice that he mainly wants to be listened to — even if it is in court. Job is nevertheless getting more aggressive, willing to take God to court. How many of us would be willing to do that? We would be willing if we wanted to make sure we were heard.

God seems to be a capricious, ambivalent God. It seems

he's fickle. "For no reason he wounds and wounds again, leaving me not a moment to draw breath, with so much bitterness he fills me. Shall I try force? Look how strong he is! Or go to court, then? But who will summon him?" (9:17–19).

Job is angry at the odds stacked against him. "Though I think myself right, his mouth may condemn me; though I count myself innocent, it may declare me a hypocrite. But am I innocent after all? Not even I know that" (9:21).

This is his first doubt. Up to now he has stood his ground. But finally he begins to wonder: Maybe I'm not innocent? Maybe there is something I'm not aware of? Once self-doubt descends, people either retreat or attack even more. Job does both. "As for my life, I find it hateful. It is all one, and this I dare to say: Innocent and guilty, he destroys all alike." God, apparently, is arbitrary. "When a sudden deadly scourge descends, he laughs at the plight of the innocent" (9:21–23).

Now the world is no longer safe, much less benevolent. If God is capricious and arbitrary, then everything is capricious and we want out. "It is all one," verse 21 says.

Okay, so life isn't fair

Job is saying he doesn't think morality matters because God isn't moral either. Whether you're good or bad, there is no equation. That's a point many people get to. Maybe they won't say it up in their heads, but they feel it down in the gut. And, of course, they are right. Life is not just. We're really not doing our young a favor if we paint for them a world in which fairness can be demanded or even expected. The poor and the outcasts seem to know this much earlier. That's their head start on the Gospel: Life itself has given them an understanding and acceptance of the essentially tragic nature of human life. Most of us have to learn it the hard way.

There's no logic. I think, personally, that I was spoiled to death, beginning with my mother who ran to the refrigerator to get me milk. I meet people who are five times better than I am, and it seems everything has gone wrong for them. There's no real equality despite the promises of the French and American revolutions. It seems the real revolution, which we still have trouble accepting, is the Gospel, which tells us to work for justice for others but not to demand, expect, or even need it for ourselves. That is extraordinary freedom.

Job is intensely struggling with this unjust world and unjust God. He speaks the truth: Dammit, it isn't right! It isn't fair. The people of the Third World, handicapped people, racial and sexual minorities have to face this very early in life. They feel it as Job is feeling it. It is not a theoretical issue for them; often it is the "hole in their soul" that never stops bleeding.

I'm struck repeatedly by how different the Gospel comes across when you preach it to someone with a full stomach and when you preach it to someone with an empty stomach. That's why Jesus said the Gospel has to be preached first to the poor (Luke 4:18–19). They're the ones who hear it rightly. Then they have to hand it on to us who don't know that we are poor.

When you preach the Gospel to sated and satisfied people, they don't understand it. They distort and misuse it for their own ego-centered purposes, their own control purposes, their own religious purposes, whatever their intent may be. They have not yet been initiated into giving up control, which we now find is at the heart of all traditional initiation rites.

The Gospel, in short, has to be preached to people like Job. They are the only ones who can hear it and not rearrange it for their own purposes. The Jobs of history have been initiated into the essential human paradox: We learn by letting go; we grow by giving up.

Toward the end of chapter 9 Job seems to have gone so

far out on a limb that he has nothing to lose. It doesn't seem to matter to this God whether one is innocent or guilty. Job has already criticized God, so now he's going for broke. He's going to let God have both barrels.

Spouses, friends, and others who get into arguments probably recognize this predicament, when they lash out at the other party and tears probably flow and they say reckless things. That's about where Job is with God.

Let's quote the whole section to feel his rage: "If I resolve to stifle my moans, change countenance, and wear a smiling face, fear comes over me at the thought of all I suffer. . . . If I am guilty, why should I put myself to useless trouble? No use to wash myself with snow or bleach my hands pure white; for you will plunge me in dung [and the original word was probably more graphic] until my very clothes recoil from me.

"Yes, I am man, and he is not; and so no argument, no suit between the two of us is possible. There is no arbiter between us, to lay his hand on both, to stay his rod from me, or keep away his daunting terrors. Nonetheless, I shall speak, not fearing him.

"*I do not see myself like that at all.* Since I have lost all taste for life, I will give free reign to my complaints; I shall let my embittered soul speak out. I shall say to God, 'Do not condemn me, but tell me the reason for your assault.' Is it right for you to injure me, cheapening the work of your own hands and abetting the schemes of the wicked?" (9:27–10:2).

If God made Job, God must be a sadist to treat his own handiwork so badly. In 10:4–5 one could almost recognize a crying demand for the incarnation: "Have you got human eyes, do you see as humankind sees? Is your life mortal like man's, do your years pass as men's days pass?"

Humanity has probably always felt this about God — "You don't understand!"

Perhaps so many people shouted at God for so many centuries that God had to become human. He got tired of that complaint, everybody saying, "You don't understand what it's like to be a human being." So God said, "Okay, I'll prove to you that I do." And he took on the body of Jesus. (Actually theologians like Duns Scotus and mystics like Meister Eckhart said it was exactly the opposite: Jesus was the first idea in the mind of God and all else is created in imitation of him.) Next Job accuses God of playing the omnipotent and dishonest court lawyer: "You who inquire into my faults and investigate my sins, you know very well that I am innocent and that no one can rescue me from your hands" (10:7). Job is innocent but God is in charge.

In chapter 10:8–12 there is a beautiful description of a tender kind of creation of which Job knows he is a part. He breaks back into his conciliatory mode: Lord, "your own hands shaped me, modeled me; and would you now have second thoughts and destroy me? You modeled me, remember, as clay is modeled, and would you reduce me now to dust? Did you not pour me out like milk, and curdle me then like cheese?"

This is playing on a Hebrew understanding of biology according to which we curdle, as it were, inside the mother's womb. "You clothed me with skin and flesh, and wove me of bone and sinew, and then you endowed me with life, watched each breath of mine with tender care."

These last verses are in stark contrast with what he was saying before. Here is a man willing to feel and experience the whole breadth of human emotion in ten verses, from rage and defiance to the most sensitive and gentle understanding of their relationship. Now that's a lover. That's a truster. That's a believer. He's living a life in defiance of the evidence. He's able to embrace all contradictions because of a deeper ontological mooring.

You "watched each breath of mine with tender care." Job is determined to claim, or reclaim, that tenderness. He cannot understand why God is no longer showing such caring, but he believes it will return.

This is an extraordinary parable of faith. There's nothing comparable in the entire Bible. The life of Jesus is, as it were, a living out of the pattern of Job. Job is the story, written in long and poetic form, and Jesus comes and lives it. Jesus, as Hebrews says, "was tempted in every way we are... but never sinned" (4:15).

But even fervent acts of faith do not always last when we are suffering. Job soon embarks on another round of self-pity. "Relentlessly your fresh troops assail me. Why did you bring me out of the womb? I should have perished there, unseen by any eye, a being that had never been, to be carried from womb to grave" (10:17–19). He seems at his wits' end and incapable of sustaining faith.

The best parallel with this tussle might be the final marriage fight before a big divorce — "You loved me once; you betrayed me; you said things you shouldn't have; I can't take your lies any more. Get out of my house."

And Job to God: "The days of my life are few enough. Turn your eyes away, leave me a little joy."

Those who have never been betrayed by someone they loved probably cannot feel this. If you have never been rejected by a friend, all this might feel histrionic and overdone.

"Leave me a little joy, before I go to the place of no return, the land of murk and deep shadow, where dimness and disorder hold sway, and light itself is like the dead of night" (10:20–22).

If we were to diagram this story, we have reached what feels like the nadir, Job's "heart of darkness."

His greatest anger seems to be in response to the masquerade of religious orthodoxy. It is also helpful, I think, to see that it is not a straight line down nor is it a straight line in return. The text, like life, is much more of a spiral.

And now, some useless common sense

In chapter 11 we encounter the third counselor, Zophar. His is the appeal to conventional wisdom and common sense, admonishing Job to pull himself together, get off his high horse, cut out all those dramatics, and get real. This is the third common counterfeit for biblical faith: the way everybody thinks.

Zophar, too, has his retributive justice theology down pat, and he does not want it to be challenged or changed. "Is babbling to go without an answer? Is wordiness in man a proof of right?" Just because he's a smooth talker doesn't mean Job is right. "Do you think your talking strikes men dumb? Will you jeer, with no one to refute you?" (11:1–3). He's saying, in effect, "I'm going to prove you wrong. You're saying you are faultless and free from blame. But 'everybody knows' it's common sense, the facts speak for themselves."

We can imagine Job rolling his eyes as if to say, "Here we go again." But his friend is already on a roll: "Can you claim to grasp the mystery of God? It is higher than the heavens. What can you do? It is deeper than Sheol. What can you know?" (11:8). He's calling on Job to believe and trust. Job, on the other hand, would like to tell him, "Believe me, I'm trusting God right now, if only you could see it. But I'm not going to trust in a lie."

God "detects the worthlessness in man," Zophar goes on, "he sees iniquity and marks it well." If we have not a warm and personal relationship with God, we will inevitably have a negative view of our humanity, as these three men illustrate. We will similarly have a cold relationship with other people, with all of humanity. In my experience there is a strong correlation between one's God-image, one's world-image, and one's self-image.

God "sees iniquity and marks it well," drones Zophar. That negative understanding of human nature returns in every age. There is still a lot of it around today. Many people feel, for some strange reason, that if they should be positive about human beings, this would take something away from God. Today it is named "secular humanism" and treated as if it were a heresy. There is no logic to it at all, but some people love to be cheerleaders for God and damners of human nature. A sure sign of an inconsistent or even unhealthy belief system.

From my first days as a Franciscan, we were told that we were "Christian humanists." I glory in being a humanist. I have no problem seeing the goodness in people as a true mirror of the goodness in God. For me, there is a direct correlation. To say "that's just human" has been turned into a condescending or pejorative comment, a put-down.

We are reflections of the invisible God (Gen. 1:27). And our only way to know God is through this humanity. This is our only road to a little enlightenment — it's called the inductive method, or for Christians the way of incarnation. We begin *here*. If I'm created in the image and likeness of God, then anthropology might be just as important as theology to understand the mystery of God. (Scholars such as René Girard and Gil Bailie are doing groundbreaking work in this area.)

We must never think we are building up God by putting humanity down. We would, instead, be insulting God, blaspheming, to set ourselves against God's creation. Paul's insight is very clear: "Ever since God created the world his everlasting power and deity — however invisible — have been there for the mind to see *in the things God has made*" (Rom. 1:20). As Tennessee Williams put it, "Nothing truly human is abhorrent to God."

But old Zophar is not there yet. "Come, you must set your heart right, stretch out your hands to him." Come on, Job, Zophar carps, admit you're wrong. "Renounce the iniquity that stains your hands, let no injustice live within your tents." Again, he makes Job the promise of a return to prosperity: "Your life, more radiant than the noonday, will make a dawn of darkness. Full of hope, you will live secure, dwelling well and safely guarded" (11:13–14, 17–18).

By coincidence Zophar also speaks in prophesy, so what he says is all true: Job's full life will indeed return, but not in the way Zophar figures it.

At the beginning of chapter 12, Job is again trying to

respond. He begins with biting sarcasm, probably understandable after such relentless harassment: "Doubtless you are the voice of the people, and when you die wisdom will die with you!" He is tired of good and sensible advice.

Job, just now, might wish it were otherwise, but he has no doubt that God has all the power. He's experiencing total powerlessness and descends to a bit of mean-spirited deflating of his advisers: "As for you, you are only charlatans, physicians in your own estimation. I wish someone would teach you to be quiet—the only wisdom that becomes you" (13:4–5).

Sometimes when we run too quickly to God's defense, as Zophar does, we miss God entirely. Zophar symbolizes the person who has conventional religious answers but refuses to seriously involve himself in a struggle with the questions.

Here in chapter 13 the author is reminding the so-called righteous not to be overzealous about defending God so quickly, and not to think they are necessarily doing God a favor by answering for God too glibly. People need to live with the mystery. They need to flow with the current. They are not serving truth or love when they push the river. God is invited and waited for, but never imposed.

Many thinking people no longer take facile Christianity seriously because they've seen how people deny their human experience and rush headlong to claim that "God has all the answers." God honors and uses our human experiences in *our* favor, so why should we do any different?

Yes, we know Christ is the answer, but what are the questions? People concerned about both the questions and the answers are full and believable Christians. But not people who, before they have thought or felt or suffered, quickly say, "God is the answer." How is God the answer? That's the question we have to allow the world if we are going to be taken seriously.

Many who go diligently to church, who read the Bible, sing hymns, are still terribly lost in hatreds and fears. They have answers but they have not struggled with the questions.

And what is the question? Or questions? Job's questions might well be our own: Is God for us or against us? Is God loving? Is it an indifferent universe? A benevolent universe? Or a toxic and dangerous one?

When we struggle with these questions, we share Job's struggle — and perhaps the inner struggle of everyman and everywoman. The one answer that seems to be clear in this book is that our distance from God is somehow also the distance we keep from our pain.

Chapter 5

Truth Is the Best Ally of God

THE MORE DEEPLY we enter into the mystery of Christ, the thinner becomes the line between joy and suffering, according to people who have gone down that road. Such people sometimes have to think twice to realize whether they are feeling joy or sorrow. Once the heart has surrendered, the only important question becomes: Are we doing God's will? Whether it brings us personal happiness or sadness is no longer of primary importance.

Job at this point is still feeling sadness, yet in the midst of his sadness he breaks through to praise and joy. But the joy is achieved through the sadness, not by avoiding it. He finds the seeds of joy in and through the sorrow. Such joy is indestructible. Christians would call it the eternally risen Christ.

In chapter 13 the author is telling us we need not tell half-truths for God's sake. We need not be defenders of God, who does not need our defense. Some religious people see their role as defending the rights and person of God. Much of this is praiseworthy, but our words will not really defend God if we do not also live the truth.

Simone Weil, the renowned Jewish thinker, was a great lover of Christ. Yet she never entered the church, although her writings are filled with wisdom and great love for God. She says, "If I had to choose between loving Christ and loving the truth, I would choose to love the truth, convinced that if I am truly seeking the truth, I will eventually fall into the arms of Christ."

In her lifetime, Weil goes on, "I have seen far too many

people who love Christ but do not love the truth. Therefore I question if they really love Christ." The Christ such people boast about is largely a projection of their own imaginations. They say they love Christ, but it becomes gradually more apparent that they are worshiping a totem called Christ but their personal and cultural agenda are really running the show. Truth, by contrast, demands a constant surrender of the self. We know we have met a great Christian who loves the truth if he or she is willing to sacrifice self and jettison personal and cultural prejudices for the sake of the truth.

The words "Lord, Lord" are being shouted far too casually in our time. "Jesus" has become a most common word on cable television. It is not countercultural in America to be for Jesus. It is quite fashionable in many circles.

The kind of civil religion in which there is hardly any difference between culture and "Christ" has few credits to show for itself in all of history. Instead it produces holy wars, anti-Semitism, crusades, and inquisitions. Even today, it is hard to find the Christ who stands apart from culture and easy to find the Christ who identifies with what everybody else is into: law and order and scapegoating of the problem people. We use the image of Jesus to hold together a disintegrating culture instead of following Jesus to build a new one based on justice and truth.

It means nothing to speak the *name* of Christ. What counts is the reality of the mystery of Christ, which is sometimes understood and lived better by those outside the fold. Thus the Jews praised Cyrus (Isa. 45:1), Jesus praised Phoenicians and Romans, and we are humbled by the Christ mystery in Mohandas Gandhi and Nelson Mandela.

If we are truly champions of the cross, we probably live a very simple and poor life. Yet, how many Christians signed with the cross are living such simple lives? How many churchgoers are materialists and militarists without even blushing? This is where the difference between the name and the reality leaps out at us. "It is not those who say, 'Lord, Lord'... but those who do the will of God" (Matt. 7:21).

The Bible has become another of those symbols people hide behind when looking for moral superiority or personal control. "Do you believe in the Bible?" the slogan is shouted in our faces. The Bible has become one of the primary indices by which people check out our orthodoxy, in the same way Catholics used to do in regard to the pope or Mary or the Eucharist. These become symbols, flags that we wave, and people check to see if we have the right flag. Flags and rituals get in the way sometimes. The important thing, however, is the reality the symbol is supposed to represent.

God as opponent and judge

In chapter 13:12 Job says, "Your old maxims are proverbs of ash. Your retorts, retorts of clay. Silence! Now I will do the talking, whatever may befall me. I put my flesh between my teeth, I take my life in my hands."

He is going to risk everything. He is going to talk back to God. He wants truth more than the private religious experience of Eliphaz, the orthodoxy of Bildad, or the conventional religious wisdom of Zophar.

"Let him kill me if he will; I have no other hope than to justify my conduct in his eyes. This very boldness gives promise of my release, since no godless man would dare appear before him" (13:15–16). In other words, would I risk taking on God like this unless I were speaking the truth? There's no point in lying to God.

"Listen carefully to my words and lend your ears to what I have to say. You shall see, I will proceed by due form of law, persuaded as I am that I am guiltless. Who comes against me with an accusation?" It is a rhetorical question. The answer, of course, is God, who has become his opponent in the court of law. "Let him come. I am ready to be silenced and to die" (13:19). The courtroom is ready. Job is taking on God as both opponent and judge. And yet also friend. The whole setting is awesome and hard to even grasp.

Seek internal, not just external authority

Job has immense inner authority. It's all any of us have: the conviction that we are who we say we are. Conventional religion has trained us to rely on external authority, which often does nothing for God or the coming of the kingdom. The promise of the Spirit is the promise of inner authority, or "power" (Acts 1:8). Many good people are taught that to trust and believe in God means to trust and believe in things extrinsic to oneself. Fortunately, when we do find healthy inner authority it is also in religious people who are calmly but utterly grounded in God.

In the Catholic tradition people tend to put their trust in the hierarchy. What does the church say? they ask, forgetting that they are the church. In the Protestant tradition they're looking to the Bible. Both church and Bible are fonts of truth and ought to be profoundly respected, but they are one step removed from the inner testimony of the Spirit. We can't avoid that responsibility.

The Spirit confers the gift of inner authority. Only people of inner authority, like Job, will use the outer authority correctly. Otherwise, people use external authority as an excuse not to walk the inner journey and discover their own souls. The church is filled with people who are living on hearsay, who stand on someone else's authority, but do not know what they themselves know. There is no "I" there to believe in God.

Whom have *you* met? Whom are *you* speaking for? What do *you* think? What have *you* experienced as the truth? What is goodness? What is evil? What is life? What is justice? What is injustice? "Well, so-and-so says this, another author says that." But what do *you* say? As Jesus said to Peter, "Who do *you* say I am?" (Matt. 16:15). Note that he took him into foreign territory, outside his usual mirrors, to ask him this personal question. We probably need to start with a reliance upon expertise, tradition, the elders (rebelliousness gets us nowhere either) but eventually God calls us into this kind of daring self-trust and self-risk that we see in Job.

Jesus wouldn't make a saint today

It is an act of courage, an act of faith, to trust our own experience. I think we are afraid of being wrong. But there's nothing so terrible about being wrong. It's the story of the entire Bible, and in that it is very different from most "lives of the saints" and church pronouncements. By our twentieth-century Roman Catholic definition of sanctity, of who should get canonized, I can't think of a single person in this book who would make it through the canonization process. Not even Jesus. The Bible, like life itself, is a "text in travail" — *revealing* the tension and problem and not simply avoiding it by presenting sanitized models.

Job himself is presented as a Gentile, outside the law and the authority of Judaism. His is almost entirely the inner authority of faith and experience. We have distorted the biblical meaning of sanctity, which is a foolish, broken person who makes all kinds of mistakes but still trusts God: David in the Old Testament, Peter in the New, for example.

There is nothing terrible about making mistakes. The only bad thing is when we don't grow up because of them. When we're still making the same mistakes at fifty that we made at twenty — yeah, that's stupid. We all do it, of course, because we're all a little stupid. But more than anything else, we do it because of a lack of inner authority, which allows us to observe, name, and own the patterns we see. Mere trust in outer authority almost always creates fear-based and shame-based people, who easily resort to subterfuge or denial.

We're always pretending we're not a part of the great unwashed, imperfect crowd. We do this giant camouflage job, largely to ourselves. If only we could see our wounds as *the way through*, as Jesus did, then they would become "sacred wounds" and not something to deny or disguise. Job's wounds, for example, are right out there.

Talking to God as an equal

Job, broken and hurting, pleads his case before the Lord. In verse 13 he says, "Grant me these two favors. If not, I shall not dare to confront you. Take your hand away, which lies so heavy on me. No longer make me cower from your terror."

The first favor he asks is that they be treated as equals. Now, that's daring. He says, in effect, if this court is going to have any justice, you should get off your pedestal, God, and let's sit here and talk as equals. Stop being the dominant one while making me the submissive one, and let's talk brother to brother and friend to friend. Then arraign me and I will reply.

The second favor Job asks is to speak first: "I will speak and you shall answer me" (13:22b). He clearly takes the offensive here: "I have nothing to lose, you're already against me anyway." When you're on the bottom, you have a lot greater ability to speak the truth.

That's why the new church is coming from the Third World, the church of the poor. It's not coming from North America or Europe. We in the West are on the top, and when you're on the top you don't care that much about the truth because you're "winning" already, at least what people call winning.

But when people are oppressed, they know that the current system is not from God. They have little to lose and everything to gain by seeking justice. God is best able to reform religion and society from a place of oppression and persecution, a pattern starting with the Exodus.

Apparently God allows Job to speak first and he runs with it: "How many faults and crimes have I committed? What law have I transgressed, or in what have I offended?" We can almost hear him screaming, "Why do you hide your face, and look on me as your enemy?" (13:23–24).

God seems to be saying nothing. All Job gets back is silence. And that silence amounts to further accusation. We have all been in that situation. There's a little tension between a couple of friends. Neither one says anything. It's driving us crazy. What is she thinking? Why doesn't he say something? Silence can have a terrible power to accuse.

"Will you intimidate a wind-blown leaf?" Job goes on. "Will you chase the dried-up chaff? You list bitter accusations against me, taxing me with the faults of my youth, after putting my feet in the stocks, watching my every step, and measuring my footprints, while my life is crumbling like rotten wood, or a moth-eaten garment." The images are poetic and profound, but what we continue to hear is a man who talks *to* God (fifty-eight times altogether) while the advisers only talk *about* God. In the end, that will make all the difference.

A turning point

The author of Job next describes what we can only call a longing for immortality. At this stage he is not yet able to believe in it. But it is one of the first recognitions in the Judeo-Christian tradition that there has to be something more than this. It can't be just a few years on this earth and then it's over. "There is always hope for a tree. When felled, it can start its life again; its shoots continue to sprout. Its roots may be decayed in the earth, its stump withered in the soil, but let it scent the water and it buds, and puts out branches like a plant new set" (14:7–9).

The implication is that, if we're as mortal as we seem, we're not as good as plants. Plants die for a season and grow again, but we don't even have that potential or privilege.

"But man? He dies, and lifeless he remains; man breathes his last, and then where is he? The waters of the seas may disappear, all the rivers may run dry or drain away, but man, once in his resting place, will never rise again. The heavens will wear away before he wakes, before he rises from his sleep. If only you would hide me in Sheol, and shelter me there until your anger is past" (14:10–13).

This is one of the more memorable sections of the book. Job is contemplating death, lamenting that things are all passing away, and reflecting, "Well, Lord, I know there is a part of you that seems to be angry, and I don't understand that. But I know there's another part of you that loves me." So Job is appealing to that second part. He suggests, as we might with our more evolved lingo, "Can't you just put me away in Limbo for a while? Put me away until you get back in touch with that better part of yourself and you're not mad at me anymore."

Then he imagines God "fixing a certain day for calling me to mind" (14:13). I have friends like that. They'll write me a note and say, "Thursday afternoon, think of me." Or, "When you're over in this other country, look at the moon on Friday night, the 21st, and I'll be looking, too." Those are ways we make connections with people we love. We move into a place where we can be one.

That is what Job is asking of God. "For once a man is dead, can he come back to life? Day after day of my service I would wait for my relief to come." I know, Lord, you love me. I am willing to wait. "And when you call I will answer. I know you would want to see the work of your hands once more" (14:14–15). How trustful, childlike, and lovely.

We can almost hear him add, "Wouldn't you?" He's pressing his case. "You've got to love me." This is the undying faith of Job, and maybe the turning point of the narrative.

"Now you count every step I take, but then you would cease to spy on my sins. You would seal up my crime in a bag, and whiten my fault over" (14:16–17). It is a beautiful statement of hope. When we are feeling overwhelmed by our guilt, on those days we feel inadequate, when our littleness and brokenness seem too much to live with, when we may even get to hating ourselves, that is when we should get in touch with the humble Job within all of us.

When you are feeling abandoned, pick up Job's book and speak Job's prayers and know they have been prayed before and that we are part of a great history and we are all in this together. There are no feelings we feel that others have not felt before. At such times, in our prayer, we unite ourselves in solidarity with others who suffer and who have suffered before us.

Often, that's the only way out of self-pity and a preoccupation with our own feelings. We have to choose solidarity and the "communion of the saints." There, we realize we are carrying the weight of our brothers and sisters, and they are carrying ours.

We get to heaven on shoulders of others

There is a weight of evil, but there is also a weight of glory (2 Cor. 4:18). We come to God by bearing one another's burdens and sins, but also by standing on the shoulders of one another's holiness and carrying one another's goodness. That is a very difficult truth for Westerners to understand.

We come from a tradition of individualism. Autonomous individuals have a sense of themselves as apart, as separate. In Africa on the other hand, they immediately understand, because the African mind thinks first of the tribe, thinks first of the people, and only secondarily of the individual. We think first of ourselves as separate and desperately try to become a part of the people, but we scarcely know how to do it.

That's why community is so difficult to form in our world, whereas community is taken for granted among most other peoples, who operate out of a corporate self that we for the most part have lost. This has done untold damage to our capacity to understand and live the Gospel.

We are psychologically preoccupied with our own hurts,

insecurities, and fears, which is the price we pay for the over-individuated self. The burden of protecting this fragile self now rests totally on us as individuals. Without God-union we have a very insubstantial self that is always needy, and finally untrue.

When I celebrated liturgies in Africa, some years ago, the liturgical instruments used were mostly percussion, drums of every tone and type, and rattles, until after a while the whole church seemed to be vibrating, everyone and everything moving.

I remember, for example, a cathedral in Kenya. The center aisle looked like "Soul Train." They don't have to become charismatics; they are naturally charismatic. I put my fingers in my ears for a moment so that I could not hear the sound. I just looked at the movement. The whole church was an undulating wave. They were so in sync, their bodies were so in union, it was amazing.

But if you come back and watch "Soul Train" in America, the participants are all emphasizing their own movements, their own individual statements, over against everybody else. Each of us is trying to assert individuality. Because we're so unsure of that individuality, we have to keep proving to everybody that we're special.

Those who know they are part of a people, like the tribal Africans, don't need to prove they are special because their significance comes precisely from their relatedness to their brothers and sisters, not their apartness from them.

This is the world of Job. Even in the midst of his anger he can easily move back into communion. He can have the courage to express his anger because he is, first of all, in communion.

This has many implications for our prayer life. Prayer is difficult for Westerners because, every time we come back to the chapel, to our prayer space, we are trying more than anything else to reestablish a communion that appears to have been lost.

It is a major task for most of us to get back in harmony,

to experience the stream of life flowing through us, of which we are only a part.

Job's moods on a yo-yo

After his surge of hope, Job ends chapter 14 with a relapse into fatalism: "But no! Soon or late, the mountain falls. The rock moves from its place, water wears away the stones, the cloudburst erodes the soil; just so do you destroy man's hope" (14:18–19).

This is a prize passage for naysayers, those people who want to take one line from scripture and make it their whole teaching. Here God is called the destroyer of man's hope. You can always take one line and prove whatever you want from it. "You crush him once for all, and he is gone. You mar him, and then you bid him go." He represents humanity saying to God, "Get out of my life." This narrative of fits and starts and backsliding is itself a teaching of hope. The firm and pious "The Lord gives, the Lord takes away" that we heard in chapter 1 is frequently recalled and retested throughout the book. Clearly conversion, which is forever refining the most intimate nature of our experience, is a long, long process. More a long road to Emmaus than a one-time road to Damascus.

Round two

In chapter 15 we embark on the second series of speeches from Job's advisers.

It doesn't seem like Job's friends are growing up much or learning a lot. Their criticisms and advice are becoming hackneyed and old hat. Eliphaz, however, is more aggressive in round two. He is thoroughly angry at Job for daring to defend himself against God: "Does a wise man answer with airy reasonings, or feed himself on an east wind?" This remark is filled with irony. From our perspective it is Eliphaz who seems full of empty talk.

"You do worse. You flout piety. You repudiate meditation in God's presence. A guilty conscience prompts your words. You adopt the language of the cunning. Your own mouth condemns you, and not I. Your own lips bear witness against you" (15:1–6).

If one or more of our friends were to speak to us like that, most of us would deeply doubt ourselves. How many would have the inner strength to refrain from saying to ourselves, "Maybe I'm wrong. How could I be right despite the criticisms of my closest friends?"

The only way we can find inner authority at that point is through God. When negative voices are assaulting us, from the world, from the spouse, the children, the church, none of us is strong enough to stand against them unless we are in touch with true transcendence.

Most people on this earth are victims of other people's mirroring. We accept the evaluations of mothers, fathers, relatives, and friends as true. I recall a fine-looking young man in our community who once heard his mother say to aunts and uncles that he was the least good-looking of her children.

He remains convinced all these years later that he is ugly. He has a lovely wife now, and everybody is quite attracted to him, but down here in the gut, where the negative voices take over, he is certain that when people look at him they think he is ugly. Until we are grounded in a transcendent reference point, we are almost totally subject to others' evaluation of us. We cannot live from within by ourselves, at least not for very long.

All poor Job can do is keep going back to God for the truth, because he cannot get it from his friends. "Are you the firstborn of the human race?" Eliphaz asks. "Were you brought into the world before the hills? Have you been a listener at God's council, or established a monopoly of wisdom? What knowledge have you that we have not, what understanding that is not ours, too? A gray-haired man and an ancient are of our number; these have seen more summers than your father" (15:7–10). Who could resist such critical nagging? Most of us don't.

Emphasize the positive

Note, again, the negative view of humanity. Negative anthropology is not necessary for a positive theology: We don't have to put down humanity to defend or exalt God. "How can any man be clean? Born of woman, can he ever be good? In his own holy ones, God puts no trust, and the heavens themselves are not, in his eyes, clean. Then how much less this hateful, corrupt thing, humankind, that drinks iniquity like water?" (15:14–16). It is a terribly unflattering image of humanity that Eliphaz has.

Visiting Germany, one can still observe some of the bad effects of Luther, who said some good things, but also some dumb things. One of the dumbest things he said was that humankind was simply a pile of manure. And Christ was the snow over the manure. He's defending Christ, saying Christ is redemptive snow, but who wants to be a pile of manure under Christ's grace? That doesn't even say much for God as creator. The Calvinist tradition veered in much the same direction. We are "totally depraved," Calvin said.

We Catholics have also made mistakes and gone down a lot of dead ends in our theology, but we have the most positive image of human nature of all the Christian traditions. One can see this in such countries as Italy or Spain, where the Catholic ethos still lingers in the daily life of the people. "Wherever the Catholic sun does shine, there is singing and dancing and good red wine," says an old English poem.

Sometimes we go too far in the direction of "eat, drink, and be merry," but it's preferable to more Nordic and Protestant countries where one often sees a dour, moralistic Christianity that always presumes the worst about human nature, is always afraid of pleasure, of doing something wrong.

For all that they gave our church, this unfortunately is also true of the Irish. They were affected by the Northern European mind, which is always protesting, it seems. But at least they protested mostly against themselves! It's an ethos that's very afraid of believing in the goodness of human nature; afraid of trusting; afraid to step up and say, "Yes, we're broken, yes, we're sinful, but we're good and we can trust that goodness and enjoy it." Perhaps the Irish best express the very tension between the two extremes: self-doubt and celebration anyway.

"Listen to me," Eliphaz goes on. "I have a lesson for you. I will tell you of my own experience, and of the teaching of the sages, those faithful guardians of the tradition of their fathers" (15:17–18).

Eliphaz is posing as a conservative. But just because we present ourselves as conservative does not mean we are in touch with the tradition. The "tradition" might be no more than some recent patterns for which we can find a few justifying quotes from the past.

Our greatest strength is to be true traditionalists, to go all the way with the tradition and find the entire pattern. The whole broad, deep, rich pattern. True Catholicism should be *kata holon:* according to the whole. The essential charism of the Catholic Church is precisely catholicity, even if we don't always achieve it.

"Catholic" could be translated as "universalist." Our word today is "holistic." This means the whole picture, not just one century or one cultural experience. What is God saying to the whole of humanity? Catholicity is still, along with our positive anthropology, the greatest strength of the Catholic Church: We have the possibility of drawing from all the sciences, countries, and centuries, and putting all that wisdom together. For all our neuroses about control and the body, Catholicism is still the most successful multicultural institution on the earth.

When we meet a true Catholic, we meet a person who is both grounded and inclusive. We do not meet a lot of them — most so-called Catholics are not catholic, they're ethnic, or they're provincial, or merely American. True Catholics have moved beyond their cultural prejudices. They include all the ages, not just the twentieth century. They put all the accumulated wisdom together and they emerge as extraordinary people.

People such as Thomas Merton or Dorothy Day or Mother Teresa are larger than life. They come out of this enormously deep Catholic tradition. They are always universal people. You cannot identify them with any one country or culture. They're bigger than any partial Gospel and they don't defend one little theology. After all, we started with at least five different theologies that today we would see as inconsistent: Matthew, Mark, Luke, John, and Paul.

Job has it up to here with his friends

Job is always gracious enough to answer, no matter what kind of trip these friends lay on him. But as he responds at the beginning of chapter 16, it's clear he's getting worn out and frustrated.

"How often have I heard all this before? What sorry comforters you are! Is there never to be an end of airy words? What a plague your need to have the last word is. I, too, could talk like you, were your soul in the plight of mine. I, too, could overwhelm you with sermons, I could shake my head over you and speak words of encouragement until my lips grew tired" (16:1–5).

Between the lines he is reminding Eliphaz that he is coming from a different place: "While I am speaking, my suffering remains. And when I am not, do I suffer any the less?" His point is that whether he talks about it, whether he gets an answer or not, it doesn't matter much; he's still hurting.

It is typical of many nonsuffering people to think that just talking about it solves it. "Perceivers" on the Myers-Briggs scale think that as soon as they've talked about the problem; it's settled, and they feel no further need to do anything about it. Their attitude is: "We have solved the theological problem, now we can forget about it."

But Job lacks that luxury and reminds such comfortable people that it's harder to forget about misery when one is feeling miserable.

There is an important clue here for understanding how the Lord is converting the church today and why the Gospel must be preached first to the poor (see Luke 4:18). It is exactly what Job is saying here: Only those who are feeling empty are predisposed to understand the Gospel. They have an "epistemological privilege" according to the theology of mission.

For the first three hundred years of Christianity we could speak of the church by and large as the church of the poor. The Gospel was preached to those on the bottom rungs of society, beginning with the fishermen. It was no accident Jesus chose little, uneducated, poor people to be his followers. He knew they would understand his message. The writings of the first Christian centuries show it remained largely the church of the oppressed and the poor.

A poor church can read the Gospel

In 313, Emperor Constantine thought he was doing us a favor and made Christianity the established religion of the Roman Empire. That was called the Constantinian Revolution. Since 313, Christians have seen themselves, not as the people on the bottom, but on the top. Before that, for example, Christians for the most part were not to be found in the army. They were pacifists who had no interest in war and conquest. Those who did join were so few, they were persecuted. But a hundred years after the Constantinian Revolution, the Christians had taken over the army and were persecuting the pagans! There is a dramatic change of mind, a moving from the disestablished position to the established position.

The church in the West has looked at the Gospel and history from that superior position for more than sixteen hundred years. We became, not the church of the poor; at our best we were *for* the poor from our privileged position of the rich.

We became a middle-class and even upper middle-class church that largely avoids much that Jesus preached about riches and wealth. The church saw no problem, as most Christians see no problem today, with being fabulously wealthy, amassing huge securities and insurance and properties, and still believing that we trust in God.

That would have been inconceivable to early believers. But the early Christian spirit is equally inconceivable to most Catholics in the West today.

We have adhered to our present view from above for so long, we don't even read the Gospels correctly any more. If some passages don't fit our culture and lifestyle, we dismiss them. Hard sayings of Jesus — for example, the reference to a camel going through the eye of a needle to indicate how hard it is for the rich to enter heaven — are written off as metaphors and literary exaggeration, and ignored.

("Usury," taking interest on a loan, was grounds for excommunication for the first millennium of the church. Not buying and selling on Sunday, a practice once sacrosanct, also passed without a whisper from the very conservatives who were against the updating of the church! Don't let anyone tell you the church has not capitulated to the demands of capitalist culture.)

We have fabricated a grid to screen anything troublesome from our consciences. Psychologists say this is necessary for survival. Thus, we let in certain information and exclude unnecessary or bothersome information, things we can't deal with. Our grid has kept out an awful lot of the Gospel for that reason.

It's futile to blame individuals. Rather, the cultural movement of history eased us into today's predicament. If we are to blame anybody, it should be old Constantine, the "ascending" culture of the West, the dominant philosophy of linear progress, the false promises of both communism and capitalism.

Christianity operates best from a marginal and minority position. Some people pride themselves in being the moral majority, but Jesus was never a part of a moral majority. The Gospel can be preached most truthfully from the minority position. From there, we can't be bought off. We won't have to sell out because we have no one to whom we must prove ourselves, no one we must please. Maybe we need to be the "immoral minority"!

Jesus said the church should be the salt of the earth, and we need to remember the salt is not the food. He said we should be the leaven in the bread, and the leaven is not the whole bread. The church, along the way, started thinking it was the whole bread, the whole food, but we're just salt and leaven. When the church operates as a small community of rooted and committed believers, then it makes a difference. From its minority position of integrity and truth, it is able to preach the Gospel. And that leaven is enough to "save" the world from self-destruction.

Here is Job, a little nobody who stands on the truth. From that position of truth he is able to call centuries of the church to the authentic, undiluted Gospel. Yet Job is barely found in Christian art, theology, or literature until this century (for example, Robert Frost, Archibald MacLeish, Gustavo Gutiérrez, William Safire, Carl Jung). This tells us that human consciousness has really not been ready for his enormous leap of disinterested faith. Perhaps the *billion* murder victims of the twentieth century have at last readied us for Job's struggle and the passion of Jesus.

For sixteen hundred years we have had the church *for* the poor. It was always thought grand and glorious that our saints and religious founders would go and help the poor. We thank God for Mother Teresa. But most of the rest of us felt entitled to live undisturbed in our established and wealthy private worlds.

A wonderful conversion is now happening in all the churches. Unable to become the church *of* the poor, we at least are trying to be the church *with* the poor. We are learning to stand more in solidarity with the outcasts of society and also to enjoy their privileged position in hearing the word of God.

Every real saint eventually left the system of possessions, privilege, and power, so that he or she could hear and speak the truth. In doing so, they were joining Jonah in the whale, Jeremiah in the cistern, Job on the dunghill, and Jesus on the cross. It seems to be the way.

Chapter 6

Job's Long Leap of Faith

IN THE SPIRITUAL REALM there is no such thing as triumph by force, even if the force is elegantly disguised by means of shame, social pressure, Vatican mandate, or political intrigue. Domination is domination and not growth, grace, or integration. The terror and wonder of the Book of Job is that God slowly allows Job to walk through the stages of grief and dying, while admittedly holding his feet to the fire.

We watch his soul unfold chapter by chapter. The text does not reveal a man becoming smaller and tighter, but instead a man growing bolder, more centered even in his anger, and more sure of who he is — even before God. That is spiritual growth by any definition.

Carl Jung distinguished between two types of suffering of the soul. First, there is "minor suffering": the little ego disappointments we must all endure as our attachments are frustrated and taken from us. The suffering of not getting our own way, not being recognized, and having to endure inconveniences. Minor suffering is a necessary school. It is the legitimate pain of being a social and limited creature on this earth. If we do not learn how to suffer legitimate pain, we ironically bring into our later life a much greater suffering of the second type.

"Great suffering" is symbolized in mythology and scripture either by sword or blood. It is the intense pain, always resisted, of realigning oneself with the real, with the totality. If there has been no practice in the school of minor suffering, it is likely impossible to jump into great suffering. If one has lived one's entire life in an autonomous and egocentric fashion, apart from union, any regrafting to the original vine will feel especially like pruning rather than growing (John 15:1–6). It will feel like death rather than life, even though it is precisely the death of who we are *not*—the false self. We all must suffer this death in one form or another.

What we see in the Book of Job is a journey through both minor and great suffering—detachment *from* and realignment *with* combined. Hopefully, the process is slowed down and gradual in most of our lives, but it is still the process. The passover lamb of the Hebrews and the Lamb of God toward whom John the Baptist points us are still central to both testaments. The lamb symbol is precisely a symbol of innocence and purity.

The suffering of the lamb will always feel unjust and uncalled for. Yes, we know bad behavior and "not being nice" must be killed in us, but actually that is not the main problem. One can be very nice and rather good, but still live independently and autonomously with oneself as the primary reference point. This is the great lie that must die, and that never dies without a major struggle. It is the good lamb that must die.

The first Copernican revolution that even the church could not accept was that our earth was not the center of the universe. This was our cosmological humiliation. The second Copernican revolution, I believe, will be when we discover that our private selves are not the center either. This is experienced as an even greater humiliation. Job and Jesus are showing us that there is a way through, a pattern, and a God who saves.

The suffering servant

In the New Testament Jesus is identified as the Suffering Servant. In fact, it is by far his most common way of referring to himself. But Job too is portrayed as a suffering servant.

Jesus becomes the new Job, the one pleading for justice from God, pleading that God will defend his case.

From stories like that of Job we can see how the Jewish scriptures were preparing us to understand the mystery of Jesus. When we have studied and prayed our way through the Book of Job, we're much more prepared to understand the passion of Jesus.

In 17:12–15 Job seems to be sinking into despair, but it is rather a resignation. This is again parallel to Kübler-Ross's description of the stages of dying. Job moves forward but only after he reaches a pit and then, finally, surrenders.

"Night, they say, makes room for day, and light is near at hand to chase the darkness. All I look forward to is dwelling in Sheol, and making my bed in the dark. I tell the tomb, 'You are my father,' and I call the worm my mother and my sister. Where then is my hope? Who can see any happiness for me? Will these come down with me to Sheol, or sink with me into the dust?"

Some of the strident harshness is gone. It is the beginning of resignation. But even the resignation does not last long.

In 19:8–12 Job is fearing that God is, in fact, treating him as an object: "He has built a wall across my path which I cannot pass, and covered my way with darkness. He has stolen my honor away, and taken the crown from my head. On every side he breaks through my defenses, and I succumb. As a man a shrub, so he uproots my hope. His anger flares against me, and he counts me as his enemy. His troops have come in force, they have mounted their attack against me, laid siege to my tent."

Then he fears the same from his family and friends. We can feel his isolation, everybody cutting him off. "My brothers stand aloof from me." There is a progressive falling away of those nearer and dearer to him. "My relations take care to avoid me. My kindred and my friends have all gone away, and the guests in my house have forgotten me. The serving maids look on me as a foreigner, a stranger never seen before" (19:13–15).

It's a magnificent description of the heart that feels lonely and isolated, something everyone has felt at times.

"My servant does not understand when I call him; I am reduced to entreating him. To my wife, my breath is unbearable. For my own brothers I am a thing corrupt. Even the children look down on me, ever ready with a jibe when I appear. All my dearest friends recoil from me in horror. Those I loved best have turned against me" (19:16–19).

There Job stands absolutely alone. "Beneath my skin my flesh begins to rot, and my bones stick out like teeth. Pity me." This line was sometimes applied to Jesus. Job is reduced to the point of begging, brought down to his knees — "Pity me, at least you, my friends," stick with me, "for the hand of God has struck me. Why do you hound me down like God? Will you never have enough of my flesh?" (19:20–22).

God and the whole world have become his enemy. He is the prototype of those who stand alone and isolated, naked before their enemies. At this verse we have come to the absolute low point of Job's journey. He is begging, desperate, and afraid.

The leap from despair

Then, at this point of absolute despair, when he has reached the bottom, he breaks through into what is perhaps the most quoted section of the Book of Job. In magnificent poetry the author has led us to an experience of the dark night of the soul and of the senses. Out of his greatest darkness comes Job's greatest statement of faith. Given the nihilism that has gone before, this is, as it were, a creation out of nothing.

Where did this faith come from? How can Job rise to the occasion like this? His resurgence is built on no obvious human foundation. There is no antecedent. It's purely a creation of grace, as faith always is. It's a being lifted up by the hair and set down in a new place to do a new thing that even surprises ourselves, like Habakkuk being carried to Babylon (Dan. 14:35–36).

"Ah, would that these words of mine were written down [now we know he's planning to say something big], would that they were inscribed on some monument with iron chisel and engraving tool, cut into the rock for ever" (19:23–24).

In this grandiose preface he is appealing to the future. He's not sure that even he can believe this now. He's not sure anybody else will believe it in the future. Humans use audio-visual aids like this when reality is getting out of control.

For example, when I'm not sure of my own prayer, I go to my journal. I want to write it so I can read it at a later time because I'm not sure that I mean it, although I want to mean it. Or I think that I mean it. Other times, when I particularly want to pray well, I go to a place where no one can hear me and I pray out loud so my own ears can hear it. I become a testimony to myself. That way, one is less likely to lie. You can't lie so comfortably when you pray out loud or when you write your prayer down.

That's the predicament Job is coping with here. He wants to believe it, he's not sure whether he believes it, but he must believe it because he's going to stake everything on what follows. He's appealing to the future, saying in effect, I'm going to chisel it in stone, to hold myself to it. He wants his trust recorded, and I think he wants it recorded largely for himself so that he'll believe it at a later date, because he doesn't know himself where this is coming from.

Verses 19:25–27

THIS I KNOW: THAT MY AVENGER LIVES,
AND HE, THE LAST, WILL TAKE HIS STAND ON EARTH.
AFTER MY AWAKING, HE WILL SET ME CLOSE TO HIM,
AND FROM MY FLESH I SHALL LOOK ON GOD.

He whom I shall see will take my part:
these eyes will gaze on him and find him not aloof.
My heart within me sinks....

In this great statement of faith every word is precisely chosen and needs to be relished: "This I know: that *my Avenger* lives."

"Avenger" has been translated variously as defender, liberator, and redeemer. These are all good for expanding its meaning.

"And he, *the Last* [the end of time; whatever this life is moving toward, somehow he's going to sum it up. Later, it will be called, among other things, the Omega point, the final chapter of history, the *pleroma,* fullness, the recapitulation of all things] will take his stand *on earth.*"

God is not taking his stand later; he's going to justify what's happening *here* on earth. He's going to protect the oppressed and the little ones now. He's going to espouse their cause. And Job dares to believe that. Sounds like incarnation or at least the dreaming of it. "After my awaking, he will set me close to him, and *from my flesh I shall look on God.*"

Note that he does *not* say he will finally know the truth or finally have justice. Job actually wants to be in relationship with God now, to "look" on him. Justice, explanations, answers, and truth are secondary, it seems, if he can be assured of mutual presence, if "he will set me close to him." The key to understanding the answer is already presented here, although most commentators and dissatisfied readers fail to see it.

He does not say from his spirit but "from my flesh." He has no understanding of his persona — whoever or whatever he is — becoming a spirit later. He is forced to accept that somehow this justification will take place even in this world; even in this life he wants to see God.

Now, that's a daring act of faith. It's the beginning of Jesus' teaching about the here-and-now kingdom of God, a kingdom that is already present. Justice somehow has to come in this world. And, of course, Job, at this point, does not believe in another world, so if it doesn't come now, it's not going to come at all. "I'm going to stand up and base my whole faith on that," is Job's assertion. Wow!

"After my awaking [whether that's a spiritual awakening or Job's equivalent of a trial time in Limbo], he will set me close to him." What trust in an intimate lover! "He whom I shall see will take my part. These eyes will gaze on him and find him not aloof" (the more literal translation is: My eyes shall see no stranger).

He trusts that his God will be a sympathetic participant, a friend, one who is *with* us and *for* us, and maybe even *in* us, but not aloof.

Then the passage lurches to a close as if the writer were overwhelmed with emotion at the truth of what he has just said: "My heart within me sinks. . . . "

From "avenger" to "redeemer"

This word "avenger," which eventually would become "redeemer," is first given to us in the Book of Numbers 35:19. Like many theological terms, it has an ordinary secular meaning. "If he has struck the person with an iron object so as to cause death, he is a murderer. . . . The avenger of blood must put the murderer to death."

The word here is *goel,* the avenger of blood. This is the victim's nearest relative. When a member of a family was killed, it was the moral obligation of the victim's nearest relative to go out and avenge with blood the blood that was shed. This protector is especially bound to prevent the alienation of the family's property, so it was at first a very worldly concept, nothing spiritual about it.

The avenger role later becomes spiritualized. We see it in Isaiah (41:14), Jeremiah (50:34), and the Psalms (19:14), until it is eventually applied even to God. The Jews came to see the Lord as one who would protect them. They saw themselves as a large oppressed family. Their enemies were killing their people, and they were such a small and powerless group they could do nothing to defend themselves, so they said, "God will be our avenger." God will be our *goel*, our redeemer. (See Rom. 12:19, which teaches that God's vengeance frees us from our need to do the same.)

This is still consistent with our belief today: the Lord as the only fitting avenger of the people. At least in our better moments, we leave vengeance and justice in God's hands.

All through this book Job has been seeking someone to defend him, to plead his case. Just a few verses back, he dared to think of God as his enemy. Now, he breaks through in this magnificent leap of faith and says, in effect, "Still I believe. I call upon God against himself. Even though God is my enemy, I also believe God will be my redeemer."

He finds truth in both sides of God and does not experience any contradiction. He bases his faith and trust on that redeemer God who will take his side, who will stand close to him, whom his eyes will look upon. For Christians it is easy to see how Jesus filled this role.

Some have suggested that these verses were the original conclusion of the book. We do not know how further material was added to these manuscripts over the ages. The later chapters are very muddled, and scholars don't know for sure how to put the scribbled manuscripts together. The book was probably written in many stages, successive authors adding their contributions.

In such a scenario, this could have been an initial climax to the book, although what we regard as the inspired text today goes on for many more chapters.

So we have to endure yet more of Job's friends' sermons. While one might expect that such a magnificent act of faith would bring everybody around, it doesn't work for Zophar. He accuses Job of pride: "Towering to the sky he may have been, with head touching the clouds; but he vanishes like a phantom once for all, while those who saw him now ask,

'Where is he?' " (20:6–7). Great faith probably looks like arrogance or delusion to those outside its pale.

Zophar nails Job for pride and more

Zophar is describing the proud man, with the implication of course that Job answers the description. For most of the rest of the chapter he goes on to describe the destruction of the wicked. In verses 14–18 he accuses Job of ill-gotten gains, taking advantage of someone. He is getting, in other words, what he deserves. Meritocracy is our natural way of arranging the world. In terms of religion it becomes the common doctrine of retribution, which confines God to *our* logic and our punitive worldview. Zophar cannot move beyond some kind of tit-for-tat.

The only thing these guys can understand is the merit and demerit system practiced in high schools. It may work for education, but the author of this book is insisting that God's plan is different.

Many good Christians, alas, are still there, living by the merit/demerit system of high school days. We apply our human systems to the magnificent work of God. Most people still work out of the rational model that we get what we deserve. It makes sense. But it leaves no room for mercy, does not reckon with the real meaning of God's love, which is not a merit and demerit system.

It's hard for most of us to adjust to: We were always told we would get what we worked for. That ethos is stamped on our psyches, it's what Dad told us. It takes a long time, therefore, for God's word to break down those emotional barriers and allow us to experience and enjoy communion with a completely benevolent God.

Many of us spend our lives as workaholics for God, hoping it will save our souls and make us worthy of God's kingdom, while God keeps breaking in to tell us worthiness is not the issue, but only relationship.

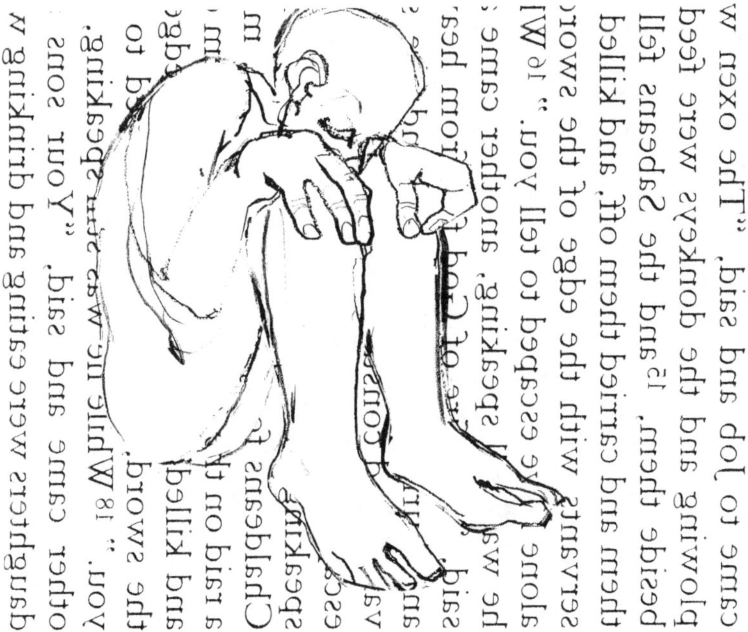

The underlying problem is that, under such circumstances, we're never going to love God. We can't love God because we won't like such a God. We're not disposed to like anybody who holds us to a merit/demerit system. As long as our parents held us at that level, we did not love them. We put up with them, had some filial affection for them, but real love cannot emerge until we move beyond merit and demerit. Why would you love God with your whole heart and soul and strength, which is the first and essential commandment (Mark 12:28–34), unless and until you know that God has first loved you in just that way?

The merit/demerit system a flop

In the rigid merit system, we know we are not loved for ourselves but for what we *do.* And as soon as we fail to do it, we are not going to get the love any more. Therefore, by definition, it's not love. Such a relation to the Lord is a trip that is going nowhere: We'll find ourselves at sixty no further in the spiritual life than we were at twenty.

I frequently see this during the retreats I give to priests and religious. They have spent their whole lives serving God but are not in love with God. And, not surprisingly, they do not have a prayer life that amounts to much. It's not, in a sense, their fault, because they were never enticed into union with God; they don't even desire such union because, after all is said and done, they ultimately don't trust God.

They are convinced God is playing a game with them. When we experience God playing a game with us, we instinctively play another game, which is called religion. "How long, O Lord?" is our attitude, "how long do we have to put up with this?" This pattern never seems to change until we encounter intimate love and are as sure of it as Job is sure.

But the good news is that we are still producing mystics. People are always falling in love with God, especially after they recognize that God loved them when they were unlovable, God trusted them when they could not trust themselves, and God forgave them when no one else would.

In verse 29, meanwhile, old Zophar concludes his self-righteous tirade: "Such is the fate God allots to the wicked. Such his inheritance assigned by God ['El']." Amen. Period. He ends with the unspeakable word the Jews used for God to close the discussion. Shut up. Hold to it and you'll go to heaven. Stop asking silly questions. This is much easier to deal with than growth and grace.

But Job comes right back in chapter 21. "Listen, only listen to my words; this is the consolation you can offer me." That's all he has been asking for since chapter 6 — "Hear me out."

"Do you think I bear a grudge against man? Have I no reason to be out of patience? Hear what I have to say, and you will be dumbfounded, will place your hands over your mouths. I myself am appalled at the thought [of what I am about to say], and my flesh begins to shudder" (21:1–6). He's amazed that what he's going to say might actually be true.

My argument, in a nutshell, says Job, is that there is no consistent pattern.

There are good people enjoying a happy life and there are good people having a miserable life — like himself. But there are also bad people who are happy and doing very well. In our less noble moments we say to ourselves about those we judge to be both rotten and rich, "They're not really happy." There's a begrudging streak in us that makes us think this way. Which raises the question: Are we living the life we do for its own sake, or because we can't do any better anyway, or because we think the unworthy rich are not really happy? (As young novices we consoled ourselves with such sour grapes.)

The rock-bottom ideal is that, even if death is the end of it all, I can still say my life is worthwhile, and I would do it simply for the truth and goodness of the action itself. It is a small and resentful attitude that wants to believe that atheists or evildoers are miserable. Which, according to our usual worldly standards, they may not be.

Job says there is no pattern. It's not true that the people who go to church are always happy and the people who don't go to church are not happy. "Why do the wicked still live on, their power increasing with their age? They see their posterity insured, and their offspring grow before their eyes. The peace of their houses has nothing to fear, the rod that God wields is not for them" (21:7–8).

He is describing the good pagan, the decent atheist. Paradoxically, it is very similar to their description of the believer. Job is turning his friends' pagan argument around, because they were using these very phrases to describe the godly — the people, as we would say, who go to church on Sunday.

"No mishap with their bulls at breeding time, nor miscarriage with their cows at calving. They let their infants frisk like lambs, their children dance like deer. They sing to the tambourine and the lyre, and rejoice to the sound of the flute. They end their lives in happiness and go down in peace to Sheol. Yet these were the ones who said to God, 'Go away! We do not choose to learn your ways. What is the point of our serving Shaddai? What profit should we get from praying to him?' Is it not true, they held their fortune in their own two hands, and in their counsels left no room for God?" (21:10–16).

In real religion, forget the old logic

Job is saying that he, by contrast, put his trust in God, and it got him nowhere. His antagonists seemingly respond that, okay, maybe some do go down to the grave apparently not suffering, but then we can be sure their children are going to pay the piper for their misdeeds.

But in verses 19–20 Job attacks that, too. He knows some children of rotten parents, and even they are doing nicely. So there's no logic to it at all, he insists.

In fact, Job goes further: It seems that God is aiding and abetting atheists, and punishing believers. "When [the atheist] has gone, how can the fortunes of his house affect him? ...One man dies in the fullness of his strength, in all possible happiness and ease....Another dies with bitterness in his heart, never having tasted happiness. Together now they lie in the dust with worms for covering" (21:21, 23, 25–26).

Job is going to be true to his experience and name what he sees happening, both the good and the bad. The three stooges are lying on behalf of God, and he doesn't think that's doing God any favor. God has to be found in the truth, and he's going to hang in there until he finds the true God — which leads him to two undeniable experiences: a benevolent God and an illogical, inconsistent, and unjust world.

Structural sins

In chapter 22 we move into the third set of speeches.

Once again, the only motive Job's false comforters appeal to for serving God is fear of punishment and hope of reward. There's not much new here; the arguments are old and hackneyed. Yet, the positions they take are approximately the same as most people take today, thousands of years later. They keep on belaboring the point because it's the conventional wisdom, the ever recurring religion. The author knows it's embedded deep in human nature. Gil Bailie calls it "the old sacrificial system" and demonstrates that the biblical revelation is forever seeking to overcome it and to make scapegoating unnecessary.

Eliphaz lists Job's sins, his "manifold wickednesses." If this is any indication of what they considered sin at that time, clearly the emphasis was on social sins, not the individual sins with which most people are preoccupied. The section is worth looking at since we still think of sin as something personal and attitudinal.

"You have exacted needless pledges from your brothers, and men go naked now through your despoiling." He's accusing Job of being an oppressor of the poor. "You have grudged water to the thirsty man, and refused bread to the hungry. You have narrowed the lands of the poor man down to nothing, to set your crony in his place" (22:6–8). Social sin is still hard for most Christians to understand, because we haven't been trained to recognize our complicity in institutional evil or what the pope calls "structural sin." It's easier to count and confess "dirty thoughts."

As long as we deal with effects or symptoms, as long as we apply Band-Aids, people regard us as religious. If we feed the hungry, that's a religious thing to do. If we give the poor money, if we heal people, if we offer them consolation, people are happy to regard us as pious and Christian and charitable.

But once we start dealing with causes, people call us political.

However, it's useless to go on indefinitely dealing with symptoms. Eventually we have to ask what is causing people to be oppressed. Or why so much of the world is hungry. This may start us talking about the role of multinational corporations. Or about the military-industrial complex. Then the alarm is raised: This is talking politically, people don't want to hear this, it's not religious. We then must decide whether we really want to look at *why* people are poor and at how we really help the poor in the long run.

If we opt to tackle the subject seriously, we must then address social sin. The problem is compounded by the fact that all of us, often unaware, are part of those social sins. No one is pure. To tackle it may mean asking our generation to question the jobs many of us are doing. Our parents' generation never considered that. When they could get a job, they took it.

Many people have found themselves out of work in recent years because, for example, they made a decision not to support the military-industrial complex. That's when faith starts getting real, when it has repercussions. It does not suffice that we be good private people if the job is immoral. We would be guilty of the sins Eliphaz is describing here.

"You have narrowed the lands of the poor man down to nothing, to set your crony in his place; sent widows away empty-handed and crushed the arms of orphans. No wonder, then, if snares are all around you, or sudden terrors make you afraid. Light has turned to darkness and it blinds you, and a flood of water overwhelms you" (22:8–11).

We are given no other evidence that these are Job's sins, but it is interesting to learn what was regarded as sins at that time. They are not merely inner attitudes but systems of which we are a part.

Excessive God talk

After accusing Job of these serious social sins, the accuser asks, "Does not God live at the height of heaven?" (22:12). This is followed by a wonderful description of God.

There's something wrong here, however. How can you argue with people once they affirm God and enroll him on their side? It puts a stop to all further dialogue. Who can be against God? And that's what these guys are always doing. They now embark on a paean of praise, of how great God is. How do you argue with that?

It's a common ploy even to this day. You're two sentences into a conversation and they pull out a scripture quote, "God said. . . ."

What they're saying is, your version of truth doesn't mean anything to us because we have this big trump card called God. The assumption is that they possess God, have God in their pocket, and thus their interpretation of this text or that truth is absolutely correct and there's no point in continuing.

This is a common occurrence. People who do it are saying they don't need you, they don't care about you, they've got their answers already, they've got their salvation without you. Because they've got God.

That's what Eliphaz is doing here. "Does not God live at the heights of heaven, and see the zenith of the stars? The clouds to him are an impenetrable veil, and he prowls on the rim of the heavens" (22:12, 14).

He goes on and on. And who could disagree with him? His point is, "I read the facts differently than Job does. I read them all in God's favor." The implication is that Job is not in God's favor. This false argument leaves Job (and us) feeling stupid and bereft of an answer, placed in the pagan position. When Christians do this to one another too quickly or arrogantly, both love and truth suffer.

Finally, in verses 21–30 Eliphaz calls Job to conversion. "Well then, make peace with him. Be reconciled, and all your happiness will be restored to you. Welcome the teaching from his lips." Of course, what he means is from *my* lips. He's taking the place of God.

"If you return, humbled, to Shaddai, and drive all injustice from your tents, if you reckon gold as dust and Ophir gold as the pebbles of the torrent, then you will find Shaddai worth bars of gold or silver piled in heaps" (22:21–25).

In other words, give away your goods in order to get other goods — he is still trapped in a materialist worldview. He's saying, trust God so you will get more. That's all. He's not a wise man.

Job answers in chapter 23. Here we see his personal search and desire for God: "My lament is still rebellious. That heavy hand of his drags groans from me." But his tone changes in the beautiful verse 3: "If only I knew how to reach him, or how to travel to his dwelling."

He does not need success. Even more than release from his pain, what Job wants is God. "If only I knew how to reach him!" He is looking for a place to abide more than an answer to his queries.

Reduced to desire

Hasn't that surely been our prayer at one time or another? If only we knew how to travel to his dwelling. "I should set out my case to him. My mouth would not want for arguments. Then I could learn his defense, every word of it" (23:4–5).

I want to hear, Job insists: What's your problem, God? I'll take note of everything you say, I'll be a good listener, God. "Would he use all his strength in this debate with me? No. He would have to give me a hearing. He would see he was contending with an honest man. And I should surely win my case" (23:6–7).

His lovely, simple belief is that God is still his friend, and he only desires to be with him.

Then we see in verses 8 and following the flip side of Psalm 139: "If I go eastward, he is *not* there; or westward—still I *cannot* see him." Psalm 139 says, on the contrary, "Wherever I go, he *is* there."

In verse 15 he goes on: "The more I *think,* the greater grows my dread of him." We should take that word "think" seriously: The more we stay in our heads, the more we create scenarios of death, logjams of contradictory ideas. The Twelve Step folks speak of "stinkin' thinkin'"!

But somehow, Job says, I can't get through to him. "God has made my heart sink. Shaddai has filled me with fear. For darkness hides me from him, and the gloom veils his presence from me." I can no longer "think God" or think it out at all. Job is being led beyond ideas and concepts to mere desire. He has been *simplified by suffering,* which is what suffering always does. He is reduced to pure desire.

What we desire enough, we are likely to get. The all-important thing is to desire, and to desire deeply. What we desire is what we will become. What we have already desired is who we are right now. We must ask God to fill us with right desire.

It's our profound and long-lasting desires that will finally explain our lives, and will soon explain Job's.

Chapter 7

Darn It, I'm a Human Being

ANY HOPE that the down-and-out may look forward to a brighter tomorrow takes a beating in chapter 24. Job, in a surprise move, states that God does not rescue the oppressed, an opinion at odds with almost all the rest of scripture, which consistently reveals a "bias toward the bottom" and an empathy for the victim.

Some would say this "preferential option for the poor" is, in fact, unique to the Judeo-Christian scriptures, and the source of its revolutionary appeal. Surely it has released in the West an innate critique of all power.

If power (religion and state) could be that wrong in the execution of Jesus and the prophets, why should we ever again presume power is right? If the victim can end up being proclaimed "Lord," we'd better be a lot more mistrustful of any creating of victims. In fact, they might be angels in disguise (see Heb. 13:2). Such biblical revelation is still turning culture and history on its head.

"Why has not Shaddai his own store of times, and why do his faithful never see his days?" Job asks. He is speaking of the Day of Yahweh, a magic day when the Lord will come and make all things right, when justice will be restored (Amos 5:18, Zeph. 1:14–18, Isa. 13:9).

Tough times for down-and-out

Job wants to know why we don't see more such Days of Yahweh. Instead, "the wicked move boundary marks away, they carry off flock and shepherd. Some drive away the orphan's donkey, and take the widow's ox for a security" (24:2–3).

The scriptures are forever reminding us that the Lord will take care of the widow and the orphan. But, Job says, there are all kinds of instances where the Lord is *not* taking care of widow or orphan. This man is not afraid to say it as he sees it. "Beggars, now, avoid the roads, and all the poor of the land must go into hiding." It sounds as topical as today's headlines, but people have always been saying it.

"Like wild donkeys in the desert, they go out, driven by the hunger of their children, to seek food on the barren steppes. They must do the harvesting in the scoundrel's field. They must do the picking in the vineyards of the wicked" (24:4–6). Job was aware, even back then, that the rich are often rich at the expense of the poor.

"They go about naked, lacking clothes, and starving while they carry the sheaves. They have no stones for pressing oil, they tread the winepresses, yet they are parched with thirst.... Fatherless children are robbed of their lands, and poor men have their cloaks seized as security. From the towns come the groans of the dying and the gasp of wounded men crying for help."

Then comes Job's clincher: "Yet God remains deaf to their appeal" (24:12). All through the scriptures God has said he would take care of them. "That's your job, God," Job is reminding him. "You're not doing what you promised. You're not taking care of the little ones." From such clear assumptions about God's role we know the Book of Job proceeds from Hebrew spirituality. Many religions would not assume this empathy for the victim.

Who are the "little ones"? Job is, on the one hand, the archetypal image of the poor man, the little man. Yet we saw at the beginning of this book that he is, by other standards, a rich man. This allows us an important clarification in regard to power and poverty. So important, in fact, that the ruling ideologies of the twentieth century, communism and capitalism, both emerge because this biblical revelation was not made clear. Let's try to let the Bible undo some of the damage.

The many faces of poverty

The world tends to define poverty and riches simply in terms of economics. That is the easiest way to look at it, and there is of course a correlation there. We need, however, to broaden that definition.

The poor person is one who either temporarily or permanently finds herself or himself in a situation of weakness, dependence, or humiliation. It is a state characterized by a lack of means. The poor do not have the means to accomplish the ends they desire.

There can be many lacks of means. It can be lack of money, or it can be in the area of relationships or influence or power or science or technology or honorable birth or physical strength or intellectual ability or personal freedom or human dignity. Lack of any of these can be a form of personal poverty — a way we are dependent or deprived, a way we feel inferior or inadequate vis-à-vis the world or those around us. The scriptures promise that God will take care of such people, because they have to rely on him, they usually have no one else. This theme is constant and unrelenting, starting with God's choice of the enslaved Semites over the empowered Egyptians.

Poor persons may themselves be to blame for their poverty to some degree, but one problem of our sophisticated age is the need to ask that question at all — who is at fault? That should not be the primary question.

As Dorothy Day once wisely said, "What the Gospel forever takes away from Christians is the right to judge between the worthy and the unworthy poor." When we sit in judgment like that, we stand aloof and apart. That's precisely the position the Gospel does not allow a Christian — as if we could critique who is worthy and who is unworthy. Our criteria will always be cultural and too often self-interested.

A person might be at fault to some degree, but poverty is primarily a psychological state to which one surrenders after repeatedly being put down. It's a state of oppression. After continually being assaulted by negative voices from within or without, finally we surrender to them. We can't stand against them. Soon we are so disadvantaged that we can't even recognize, much less take advantage of, the opportunities offered to us. The negative voices of cultural shame soon become self-fulfilling prophecies.

People who have never been in this downtrodden, impoverished situation can be very unsympathetic because they don't realize what's happening inside. From their secure position — usually in the middle or upper classes — it's easy to call the poor lazy or unmotivated. Such people do not understand the psychological dimension of poverty. The poor have little chance of changing their state without some help from outside. Some "good news"!

This state is often characterized by what is called "victim behavior." It's self-destructive and other-destructive, and it characterizes all oppressed people. Those who are not in such a state of oppression cannot understand their behavior. It doesn't fit their criteria, so they misjudge and misinterpret almost everything the disadvantaged do.

Victim behavior is predictable. It is deadly. And it characterizes much, if not most, of the human race in one form or another. We may all be thinking of some group other than ourselves, but every group finds itself in that state of oppression in relation to some other group. Women in relation to men, for example: They have a whole set of attitudes and feelings that a man can't understand without "enlightenment."

What to do with power?

One aim of St. Francis was to undo a world in which some had all the power and others had none. He writes in his first Rule, "All the friars without exception are forbidden to wield power or authority, particularly over one another" (Rule of St. Francis, chapter 5).

He forbade any titles of dominance or superiority in our community and opted to live totally outside the system of economic power and the seeking of one-upmanship in any form whatsoever. We could not even ride horses because that was a symbol of superiority and military strength.

He chose, therefore, to live upside down, to try to create, in some way, a world that is cooperative rather than competitive, based on mutual submission rather than dominance. Neither he nor anyone else has fully succeeded in this following of Jesus. But the trouble is that most of us have not even tried — not even the church.

The communists tried to deal with it, but all they did was take away power from the upper classes and give it to the state. The problem remains the same. In capitalist societies we have given all the power to the people of wealth, while calling it democracy.

I don't know if there is an answer on this earth, a secret to overcome this state of universal seeking of power. The closest approach to an answer is the Gospel: a worldview based on simplicity, nonviolence, and nonidolatry of all things except God. That puts us outside every system of control and power.

It seems that cultural structures are naturally skewed in favor of power, prestige, and possessions. That seems to be human culture at its worst, but also human culture in its universal state. Without grace, culture ("the world") seems inevitably to follow the other universal law — gravity.

"Incapacity to feed upon light"

This aspect of our human condition is best illustrated by an experiment. A wall-eyed pike is put into an aquarium. He is fed for some days with little minnows. Then, in the middle of the experiment, a glass partition is placed down the middle of the aquarium so that the pike is now confined to one side.

Then the researchers drop the minnows on the other side. Immediately, the pike goes for the minnows, but he hits himself against the glass. He circles and hits it again. He tries a third time, but he is now hitting the glass a little less hard. After a few more times, he's just sort of nosing up against the glass. He has a feeling he's not going to get those minnows. Pretty soon, he just swims around in circles and ignores the minnows on the other side.

At that point, those doing the experiment take out the glass. The minnows come right up against the gills of the pike and he doesn't even try to eat them.

The experiment ends when the wall-eyed pike starves to death. He's convinced he's not going to get those minnows, so there's no point in wasting his time or hurting his nose again. That is the best image of cultural blindness I have heard. I wanted to weep when I first heard it, but I realized that the experiment is about human beings, not about fish. That's much of the human story, people spiritually starving in the midst of plenty. They don't know how to eat.

Only the Gospel will ever be able to free their spirits so they can know how to eat and what to eat. Simone Weil puts it well: "All faults are the same because there is really only one fault: our incapacity to feed upon light."

The sadder thing is when Christians stand aloof and in judgment on their brothers and sisters because they themselves have never experienced oppression. They have always been on top of the pile and have never felt what it was like to be on the bottom. The author of Hebrews rightly warns us: "Let us go to him, then, outside the camp, and share his degradation" (Heb. 13:14).

Eventually, oppressed people form a whole subculture. These subcultures take different forms in different ages. They are controlled by predictable factors: fear, anger, guilt, prejudice, superstition, compulsive behavior, inhibitions, fantasies, fatalism, conformity, hopelessness, sexual acting out, passivity, and more.

These are the ways the spirit surrenders. It surrenders in order to survive, to make some sense out of this world when all its power has been taken away. The outsider, who is not oppressed, can't understand. The oppressed become the screen on which we project our own condition. Every group projects its fear and self-hatred onto another racial or religious or economic group. Whatever we can't deal with in ourselves, we are sure to find it characteristic of others, and hate it there. The Jewish people had a perfect symbol for it, the scapegoat: "And the goat will bear all their faults away with it into a desert place" (Lev. 16:22).

In Montana they talk that way about South Dakotans. Catholics used to do it to Protestants, Protestants to Catholics. Everybody has somebody to lay the blame on. Until we know ourselves and until we are grounded in true transcendence, we are intrinsically insecure and in search of someone to blame for our own unhappiness. Without God or with false gods, it seems humanity is inherently resentful and violent.

We are, of course, saying much more about ourselves than about the other group. We are saying that we don't know who we are. Once we know our own souls, once we find our identity in God, we don't need to scapegoat others. We are big enough, small enough, and secure enough to bear the dark side of things within ourselves. What we are watching in this story of Job is one man's journey into bigness, smallness, and utter security.

Get the poor out of sight

One outcome of the present predicament is that we despise the poor, however we may describe them. We marginalize them, push them to the periphery, try to keep away from them. The poor—today it's the mentally or physically handicapped, minorities, refugees, the addicted, homosexuals, prisoners, anybody who has failed to meet the expectations of the majority in the economic or social success system — represent what we are most afraid of and deny in ourselves.

Because we are so afraid of nonsuccess, of being a refugee, not having a home, afraid of the opposite masculine or feminine parts of our own souls, we marginalize whoever represents those parts of our soul that we deny. We hate in them what we are afraid to admit in ourselves. We keep ourselves at a distance from handicapped people because every one of us fears our own handicaps. We separate ourselves from retarded people. They're a threat to our supposedly rational world. We surround ourselves, unfortunately, with clones of ourselves.

We separate ourselves from weakness and brokenness at a loss to ourselves — maybe even the loss *of* ourselves. Job becomes the archetypal image of this truth in the Hebrew scriptures. Perhaps no one states it more precisely than St. Paul toward the end of his life: "Wherefore, so that I should not get above myself, I was given a thorn in the flesh, a messenger from Satan to batter me and prevent me from getting above myself. About this I have three times pleaded with the Lord that it might leave me; but he has answered me, 'my grace is enough for you: for power is at full stretch in weakness.' It is, then, about my weaknesses that I am happiest of all to boast, so that the power of Christ may rest upon me; and that is why I am glad of weaknesses, insults, constraints, persecutions, and distress for Christ's sake. For it is when I am weak that I am strong" (2 Cor. 12:7–10). It sounds like a testimony at a Twelve Step meeting.

When the church forgets its own Gospel, the Spirit teaches it in new forms: the first step of the Twelve Steps is to admit that you are powerless. It takes a long time to take that first step.

The many uses of religion

Sociology says that religion is now understood in at least three different ways, depending on where we stand in the economic system.

People from the upper class tend to see religion in terms of healing and spiritual comfort. They feel, deep down in their souls, that something is wrong, something is still missing in their world, so they come to God to get spiritual comfort, and they will make the Gospel, almost in its entirety, into a doctrine of inner and personal consolation. They have the physical comforts but they see these are not enough.

The middle class, from the sociological perspective, typically comes to religion for the sake of social relationships and community. They are usually so preoccupied with climbing and making more money and competing that they don't know how to relate to other people any more. They don't know how to link and bond with others. So they seek some relationships in church and community.

The little people of the world come to religion to meet survival needs. They come asking the life-and-death questions. They are not interested in disconnected theories and theologies. If it isn't real, they won't listen. They want to know whether we are working for people and whether we are loving. They can preach the Gospel back to the preacher in ways that hurt, ways we don't want to hear. My best theology school for the last nine years has been the Albuquerque city jail, where I am Catholic chaplain.

I believe that's why Jesus said the Gospel has to be preached to the poor, because they force us to deal with the survival questions of the Gospel. The middle and upper classes have played with the Gospel for too long. The over-educated clergy have distorted and misused the Gospel for our own purposes of management.

What we are discovering is that we again have to preach to the poor all over the world. The reason is not to save them for the church; not necessarily to make them into Roman Catholics; not to save them from their poverty either (which some activists think we're saying); not to make reparation, not out of guilt; not even in sympathy for their terrible plight; not even to be witnesses to generosity or nobility or our great Christianity.

Rather, the primary reason to preach the Gospel to the poor, and why the church has to get back in touch with the little ones and the marginalized, is so that the church itself can be converted; so that the church itself can know again what the questions are; so that the church itself can recover compassion; so that the church itself can discover what God is really like. So that the church can again meet Jesus.

God is not asking nor answering the law-and-order questions that culture desires from religion. Jesus never speaks about so-called "family values" or institutional loyalty, which are so often misused by people who want order and control.

God is instead asking us to discover our own souls, to save the church and to save the Gospel from any further distortion of the Gospel, to be in solidarity with weakness and truth, to surround ourselves with those sacraments of brokenness so we will have the courage to discover that we also are broken. The broken are no different than we are; they are only more visible sacraments of what we are trying to hide: our own lack of intelligence, our handicaps, our lack of a true home. Those are the deep Gospel truths we are afraid to face.

Why couldn't Jesus be rich and dandy?

The world is afraid of the poor Jesus, just as we are threatened by the poor Job. The Gospel, by contrast, teaches us how to be a shared and sharing people. On the occasions when I am able to preach in a poor country, I discover how unfree we are in our rich country. I find that we who seem to have so many possessions do not in fact possess them, but they possess us. And this poses the conundrum: Who is really free?

When I was in the Philippines I was struck by the fact that when a family kills a pig or even a small chicken, they share it. Because they can't eat it all in one night, they go around to each house with a little portion for everyone.

When I returned to America I realized we have this great technological discovery, the refrigerator, and some of us even have freezers, so we don't need to share. Is it a gift? I guess so. I have one too. But it's an ambiguous gift. And we have paid a price for that so-called gift. We don't know how to share because we don't need to share.

I noticed in Africa and Latin America that in many houses of the poor there are no doors. In our houses there are two or three doors and two or three locks. Then I see a nation fortifying itself with missiles and guns, because the more you have the more fearful you are. And the most fearful people in the world are Americans, because they have so much to lose. And never has there been a people with so much who are still afraid of not having enough. It's an addiction called greed. The more you have, the more you want, and the more you are preoccupied with protecting it. And the more you need to protect it, the less you are able to enjoy what you have.

Then I see why Jesus designated the little people of the world as free and happy. Despite the obvious pain and frequent bitterness, there is often a joy in the barrios of the world that I do not see in the middle-class world. The few options the poor do have, they have to enjoy them.

We are not constrained to enjoy anything in particular because there is always something else, another option we can exercise. Job is our teacher in more ways than we imagine. He is learning how to find joy, how to find inner freedom, when all those other things are taken away.

We Americans can call ourselves free, but I'm not so sure. I'm not even so sure that we Gospel people have discovered the true character of freedom. Political freedom of itself does not guarantee that people are actually free.

God takes away, as it were, Job's physical freedom so that he has to discover spiritual freedom. We could call the Book of Job "a tale of two freedoms." God and Job are continually freeing one another to love back in ever more perfect freedom. Perfect love demands perfect freedom.

It seems that God has so designed and ordained his church that each group needs and liberates the others. We must give our lives to liberate the oppressed from injustice. But the oppressed and poor in turn must liberate us from our illusions and our innocence.

Thus, we both need one another. No group can say, "We have the whole Jesus." Some have the luxury to take Bible courses, get degrees, buy books, attend conferences. Most of the people of this earth can't afford to have all their needs met in this way.

What are we doing with the leisure we have to study the word of God? Are we liberating others? Are we being freed from our illusions or are we simply using God to maintain them? I can't imagine that you are still reading this difficult Book of Job if you are not willing and desirous of being freed from your "unwoundedness," which is the first meaning of innocence. Such innocence is very dangerous.

Let's console ourselves with a hymn

We return in chapter 25 to one of Job's advisers, Bildad of Shuah, who, we recall, uses religious orthodoxy as an avoidance of faith. Bildad embarks on a great hymn to

God's omnipotence. There's something very lovely — and escapist — about this.

Bildad is the type of guy who, after a hard prophecy is given at your local prayer meeting, pipes up, "Let's sing Psalm 35." Everybody stands up and the tambourines start going and the word doesn't get a chance to sink too deeply.

One can always tell people who are afraid of pain. That's the kind of thing they do right away. Get it back to joy. Because they can't deal with pain. They want resurrection theology, not the whole paschal mystery.

The "mystery of faith" we proclaim at the Eucharist is precisely the whole paradoxical process. Resurrection theology without crucifixion theology is heresy, half the truth, half the Gospel. Just as an exaggerated emphasis on the crucifixion is dangerous and destructive without a belief in resurrection: Jesus is risen and suffering *now*.

Bildad nevertheless calls out his psalm of praise. He feels the need to "raise up the Lord." But especially to give himself a break.

"Can anyone number his armies, or boast of having escaped his ambushes? Could any man ever think himself innocent, when confronted by God? ... The very moon lacks brightness, and the stars are unclean as he sees them. What then of man, maggot that he is, the son of man, a worm?" (25:3–6). Once again God is praised at the expense of humans.

In chapter 26, however, we find perhaps the most accurate and poetic description of the cosmos in all the scriptures. The passage resembles Carl Sagan on television giving his description of the universe. "He it was who spread the North above the void, and poised the earth on nothingness" (26:7). That's the only hint in all of scripture of the possibility of infinite space. The writers presume, in every other description, that the world is standing on pillars, that somewhere there is a foundation to this globe, or more likely they are still thinking the earth is flat.

Nevertheless Job breaks into Bildad's lovely cosmology.

Thanks but no thanks, he fires back at Bildad. I know God's power and beauty, Job is saying in effect, but that doesn't help right now. "To one so weak, what a help you are, for the arm that is powerless, what a rescuer. What excellent advice you give the unlearned, never at a loss for a helpful suggestion. But who are they aimed at, these speeches of yours?" (26:1–4).

Job says, in essence, to Bildad: "I think you're talking to yourself, not to me. You're dealing with your own fear with regard to the poor and oppressed. You're running away from it. You're giving a speech to yourself about God's greatness, but, my friend, I'm totally convinced of God's greatness and the beauty of the world, which you would know if only you would listen."

But Job's actual words to Bildad are more direct. "I swear by the living God who denies me justice, by Shaddai who has turned my life sour, that as long as a shred of life is left in me and the breath of God breathes in my nostrils, my lips shall never speak untruth.... Far from ever admitting you to be in the right, I will maintain my innocence to my dying day" (27:1–5).

You're human but that's okay

What impresses about this chapter, however, is its courageous defense of being human. Job is defending not so much his own perfection as his humanity. He's saying, "Darn it, I'm a human being, I'm somebody." Literally, "My conscience gives me no cause to blush for my life" (27:6).

The first permission we have to give a little child when it comes into the world is the — unspoken or spoken — *permission to exist.* Many people have never been given that permission. No one has looked into their eyes and said, by whatever means of communication, "I am excited and happy that you exist. Your very being is good."

The whole Book of Job can be read in that context: a

human being demanding his rights as a human being. "Someone, tell me it's okay that I exist," is the message between the lines. People who are happy, who know freedom and enjoy self-assurance, are those who somewhere, somehow, were told by mother or father or someone, "I'm so excited that you're on this earth." Job is asking for the gift of unconditional love when he rejects any theory of retributive justice. He is demanding a God who respects and loves what God has created — just because it is.

Personally, that's the only reason I'm a preacher of the Gospel. The reason I can say soft things and hard things and be comfortable with both is because I had a mother and father who looked into my eyes and told me I mattered. They were just all excited about me for years on end. (My sister came five years after me.) So I can be excited about myself. That may sound self-centered, but it's what God wants of all people. I trust my intuition and thoughts. Most people can't do that. They're always afraid: What if they're wrong? What if their thoughts are not correct? So, often, they don't say anything. As you can tell, I just chatter on!

What Job is hoping for, and even demanding, is that God look into his eyes again as at his creation: "You modelled me, remember! As clay is modelled.... You endowed me with life, watched each breath of mine with tender care" (10:9, 12).

What he most fears is the "evil eye" that accuses and dismisses him as insignificant: "Will you never take your eyes off me long enough for me to swallow my own spittle?... What have I done to you, you tireless *watcher?*... Can you not overlook my fault?" (7:19–21).

Job is surely everyman and everywoman waiting and searching for the gaze that does not lie. It seems God alone can give it. When we know in our mirrored soul that someone is happy we exist, especially when we know God is happy we exist — it becomes a self-fulfilling prophecy. We call it eternal existence. It is a gift of seeing and being seen. I now believe that it is not so much from our "sins" that

God has freed us as from that sense of utter abasement and littleness that all human beings seem to feel before God.

A hymn to wisdom

In chapter 28 we come to what Gustavo Gutiérrez calls "the poetic hinge" of the whole book. It also serves as a graceful judgment on the nonwisdom that has been coming from Job's friends in the previous twenty-five chapters.

Wisdom is seen as the divine *immanence* "down there" in the material world (verses 6–7), already engraved in the way things are. There is a "transcendent within" to this material world, symbolized by images of ore, silver mines, and precious stones hidden in the rocks. Yet these images are immediately balanced and seemingly contradicted by other images of divine *transcendence*. " 'It is not in me,' says the Abyss; 'Nor here,' replies the Sea" (verse 14). "It is outside the knowledge of every living thing, hidden from the birds of the sky" (verse 21). "God alone has traced its path and found out where it lives" (verse 23).

As in all real orthodoxy, we find here an ideal balance between inner natural law and outer mystery. God has written the patterns in things as they are and yet we never see the full pattern without divine assistance. God seems to be both perfectly hidden and perfectly revealed in all things. Thus faith (trust in the other) is always necessary to see what is then "natural." What a paradox!

The punch line is in the final verse, which strongly asserts praxis over any theory or theology. It seems that immanence and transcendence come together not in the head but in behavior, not in clear principles but in right relationship: "Wisdom? It is fear of the Lord. Understanding? It is avoidance of evil" (verse 28). God, it seems, cannot really be known, but only *related to*. Or, as the mystics would assert, we know God by loving God, by trusting God, by placing our hope in God. It is a nonpossessive, nonobjectified way of knowing. It is always I-thou and never I-it, to use Martin Buber's wonderfully insightful phrases. God allows us to know him only by loving him. God, in that sense, cannot be "thought."

Job has become the living icon of such "praxis." The three advisers have correct theory but no experience, thoughts about God but no love of God. They believe in their theology; Job believes in the God of their theology. It is a big difference.

Chapter 8

God's Angle on Evil

JOB'S ODYSSEY is nearly over. Whether journey's end will be fulfillment or disappointment will depend on our point of view.

In chapter 29 Job describes his past, so lovely in hindsight. He was a success then, on top of the situation, admired by everyone. It is bittersweet to remember, as we all learn in later life. Now, in chapter 30, he is trapped in a different world. "Now I am the laughingstock of my juniors, the young people whose fathers I did not consider fit to put with the dogs" (30:11). There's a bit of pride still there in spite of everything, and his self-righteousness is still growing.

He complains at length about the public contempt in which he is held: "They have cut me off from all escape, there is no one to check their attack. They move in, as though through a wide breach, and I am crushed beneath the rubble. Terrors turn to meet me, my confidence is blown away as if by the wind; my hope of safety passes like a cloud. And now the life in me trickles away, days of grief have gripped me" (30:13–16).

Job as his own lawyer

Chapter 31 is sometimes described as Job's apology for his life. It seems that when a man was put on trial in the Jewish tradition, he was expected to plead his own case. This is exactly the situation we have here. Job's plea is "Not guilty."

Acting as his own lawyer, he even takes oaths, in a sort of standard form.

He goes through all the great sins of the day and each time swears he didn't do it. The sins run throughout chapter 31.

First, he declares he has not been guilty of lust: "I made a pact with my eyes, not to linger on any virgin." That's different from most Catholics, who generally keep their sins of lust for last at confession.

Next, he denies being deceitful. "Have I been a fellow traveler with falsehood, or hastened my steps toward deceit?" The implied answer to these rhetorical questions is always negative. "If he weighs me on honest scales, being God, he cannot fail to see my innocence."

And here follows the standard oath in verses 7 and 8: "If I have done this, let this happen." Thus, "If my feet have wandered from the rightful path, or if my eyes have led my heart astray, or if my hands are smirched with any stain, let another eat what I have sown, and let my young shoots all be rooted out. If I ever lost my heart to any woman, or lurked at my neighbor's door (a euphemism for adultery), let my wife grind corn that is not mine, let her sleep between others' sheets."

These are very dramatic images. He's saying, "Listen, I have not done wrong. And if I have done wrong, let these terrible things happen to me."

Next, he insists he has not been unkind. "If ever I have infringed the rights of slave or maidservant in legal actions against me — what shall I do when God stands up? What shall I say when he holds his assize? They, no less than I, were created in the womb by the one same God who shaped us all within our mothers" (31:14–15).

It is interesting how far ahead of Job's time verse 15 is. Indeed, throughout much of chapter 31 the morality is centuries ahead of its time, a profound theological statement. The author points out, among other things, the equality of slaves and free persons.

Then he says he is not guilty of injustice. "If my land calls down vengeance on my head, and every furrow runs with tears, if without payment I have eaten fruit grown on it or given those who toiled there cause to groan (if, in short, he has been unfair to his employees), let branches grow where once was wheat, and foul weeds where barley thrived. Have I been insensible to poor men's needs, or let a widow's eyes grow dim? Or taken my share of bread alone, not giving a share to the orphan?" (31:38–39, 16–17).

The implication is, of course, that he has done none of these unworthy things.

But soon we see again, in verse 18, his loving relationship with God: "I, whom God has fostered, fatherlike, from childhood, and guided since I left my mother's womb." His is a confident claim: As he was treated fatherlike, so has he done to others. "Have I ever seen a wretch in need of clothing, or a beggar going naked, without his having cause to bless me from his heart, as he felt the warmth of the fleece from my lambs?"

He defends himself against any misuse of power. "Have I raised my hand against the guiltless?... If so, then let my shoulder fall from its socket.... God's terror would indeed descend on me; how could I hold my ground before his majesty?"

He defends himself against greed. "Have I put all my trust in gold, from finest gold sought my security? Have I ever gloated over my great wealth, or the riches that my hands have won?" (31:24–25).

He defends himself against false worship, using a rather interesting phrase: "Has the sight of the sun in its glory, or the glow of the moon as it walked the sky, stolen my heart, so that my hand blew them a secret kiss?" He is denying involvement with astrology or with trusting in the sun and the moon instead of in Yahweh, the Lord of Israel. "That, too, would be a criminal offense, to have denied the supreme God" (31:26–28).

Neither, he insists, has he been vindictive. "Have I taken pleasure in my enemies' misfortunes?" Neither has he been inhospitable. "The people of my tent, did they not say, 'Is there a man he has not filled with meat?' No stranger ever had to sleep outside, my door was always open to the traveler." Furthermore, he goes on, he has never been a hypocrite. "I have never hidden my sins from men, keeping my iniquity secret in my own breast" (31:29–33).

Then, in verse 35, he wraps up his case. "Who can get me a hearing from God? I have had my say from A to Z; now let Shaddai answer me. When my adversary [he is still, when the mood strikes him, calling God his adversary] has drafted his writ against me, I shall wear it on my shoulder" (31:35–36). He is willing to take whatever God decrees, if only God would just say something. Whatever the verdict, he vows to wear it like a badge, to "bind it round my head like a royal turban. I will give him an account of every step of my life, and go as boldly as a prince to meet him." And with that he rests his case. He has challenged the divine judge. Job is either a rebel, a fool, or an utterly confident son. Probably all three.

Enter Elihu (heroic idealism)

The following chapters are almost certainly a later addition. Somebody came along, probably shortly after the original was written, maybe a member of this same wisdom school from which the Book of Job emerged, with the idea of improving the book. The later writer or writers are not satisfied with Job's three friends; they must add another. It is very likely that Elihu, the fourth speaker, reflects the personality and mind of a later author.

This later arrival seems very self-assured, even arrogant. In today's lingo we might call him the first of the angry young men. I see him as the symbol of youthful idealism and inordinate zeal which is often confused with religious faith. Elihu is like the guy at the end of a three-hour prayer meeting, after folks have sung fifty songs, made forty-seven prophecies, and had thirteen other "sharings," and everyone is dying to get out of there — this one man has to get up and talk one more time. Ego in the service of God.

Elihu is taking himself far too seriously. He thinks the whole case is going to depend on his big sharing. We will move quickly over chapters 32 to 37, however, because Elihu says scarcely anything that has not been said before. One might say that the gratuitous addition of this section reveals the author's own problem.

This superfluous section begins: "These three men said no more to Job because he was convinced of his innocence. But another man was infuriated [he is referring to himself, the later, uptight author] — Elihu, son of Barachel the Buzite, of the clan of Ram. He fumed with rage against Job for thinking that he was right and God was wrong; and he was equally angry with the three friends for giving up the argument and thus admitting that God could be unjust" (32:1–3).

So Elihu steps forward as the great defender of God. It takes Elihu all the way from 32:6 to 33:7 to build himself up. All he does is alert us by saying, "I'm about to say something really important." Talk about a big ego, as in "Get ready, get ready, I'm going to say something really important." Then, after all that presumption, he accuses Job of presumption. Heroic idealism is in the way. The first line is the giveaway: "I am still young" (32:6). What we can expect in his remarks is the success/power/image needs that invariably characterize young men. In the men's movement we call it "infantile grandiosity."

What Elihu does add to the discussion is an account of the different ways God speaks. Indeed, the next few verses constitute a rather delightful commentary on dreams.

God "speaks by dreams, and visions that come in the night, when slumber comes on mankind, and men are all asleep in bed. Then it is he whispers in the ear of man, or may frighten him with fearful sights, to turn him away from evil-doing" (33:15–17).

Carl Jung would say that dreams often reveal the shadow side of the personality. The shadow comes forward and the nightmares chase him. Why? "To turn him away from evil-doing, and make an end of his pride; to save his soul from the pit and his life from the pathway to Sheol."

Secondly, Elihu goes on, suffering is the way God speaks. "With suffering, too, [God] corrects man on his sickbed" (33:19). True for sure, but still a cliché in his young mouth.

Angels and other messengers

In 33:23 there is a very interesting passage. "Then there is an angel by his side, a mediator, chosen out of thousands, to remind a man where his duty lies." Literally the word is "interpreter" rather than "mediator." Some, especially the ancient fathers, have seen this as a promise of the "guardian angel." It is a belief Jesus seems to take for granted: "Do not despise any of these little ones, for I tell you that their angels in heaven are continually in the presence of my Father" (Matt. 18:10).

History is full of stories of people saying they met a messenger or an angel who spoke to them or guided them, so there is obviously some wonderful truth at stake here. This voice within us, in our deepest soul, says, "release him from descent into the pit [the angel is always a positive voice, never a negative voice], for I have found a ransom for his life; his flesh recovers the bloom of its youth, he lives again as he did when he was young" (33:24–25). Maybe "the better angels of our nature" that Abraham Lincoln spoke of are exactly that: They hold us to our essential self, our best self.

Our tradition says that when you take the spiritual journey you have to walk out into the wilderness, or into the desert, and there you meet the wild beasts and the angels. Jesus did it in Mark's Gospel (1:12–13). If you're willing to face the wild beasts, as Job has been doing for thirty-three chapters, you are not going to meet just wild beasts, you are going to meet the angels.

This is surely true. People who have risked facing their shadow and their inner darkness, the terror that's inside all of us, are also the people who make the most profound discoveries of their inner goodness, of the presence of the divine within them. Conversely, many people do not discover the divine presence within them because they do not risk facing their inner and outer demons the way Job did. I often wonder if there is any other way

Elihu the teacher

It is clear that Elihu is not so much talking with Job as pretending to teach him. When people insist on teaching us instead of sharing with us, what they have to say will never sink very deeply. That's the weakness of my own role as perpetual preacher. The most we teachers can do is arouse people's curiosity, make them think, blow open their systems and stir up their minds, hearts, and souls. But the people most likely to change our hearts are those who share, the people who walk with us, who love us. Those are the people we might change our lives for. We're not going to change for the likes of Elihu. As Pope Paul VI said, "The world will believe teachers only if they are first witnesses."

We know Elihu, standing in that position of superiority, is not going to help Job. "I've got the truth and you don't, Job. You're dumb and stupid. Now listen to me." We seldom listen to people like that. It's just human nature. We won't receive their words unless they come as an equal and walk with us and admit they have the same problems and the same pain we do.

In chapter 36 Elihu goes on to defend God again. "I have more to say on God's behalf." And then he tells Job the meaning of Job's suffering. "You are wretched," he says in effect (verse 15), which is the last thing Job needs to hear.

Laying guilt and shame on folks only paralyzes them. It is a common parental mode for exacting compliance, but does not last long because the soul is untouched.

Elihu is clearly the comic relief before the great climax.

Finally — God speaks up

In 36:22 Elihu breaks into a great and beautiful hymn to God's wisdom and omnipotence, which continues through chapter 37. But even God cuts him off, bored with all this superfluous flattery. We have not heard God speak since the beginning.

God says, in effect, "Aw, shut up!" And "from the heart of the tempest Yahweh *gives Job his answer*" (38:1). This is undoubtedly the most quoted part of the Book of Job. If we are not prepared for it, we might at first resent it. All this time we have been waiting for the big answer. The problem of evil in a nutshell. How is God going to get out of this one?

A surprise awaits us. In all of chapters 38 and 39 there is not a single answer. Yet the first words are, "Yahweh gives Job his answer." It is all questions. God doesn't formally answer a single one of Job's complaints. Only God could get away with this. All God does is offer a radically new perspective which makes the answers unnecessary. God invites Job into a warm and personal encounter with himself.

And it seems to work. It's as if Job jumps with glee and says, "It's okay, God, I don't need the answers anymore. I love you, Lord, and I know you love me. At last you have spoken to me. That's all I wanted. Just talk to me — I don't care what you say."

Wives and husbands especially will recognize how human this is. After a three-day cold silence, it's so good to be talking again and back in communion. That's what we feel in these chapters: Job is so excited to have God talking to him again that he no longer needs the answers.

There is a critical insight here. When the church gave us

the impression there were ready-made answers, it was doing us more harm than good. When God himself, in this great dramatic presentation, refuses to give us answers, and calls us instead into communion, that — for some nonrational, right-brain reason — is the answer. That's all we want, or need.

We want to know that someone is happy we exist, that someone is saying, "I believe in you. We're in this together." With such reassurance we can carry on.

God is characterized as living in the heart of the whirlwind, an amazing image — "Out of the whirlwind truth comes." A tornado, as it were. You can't hold this God down, you can't explain this God. This God is dynamic, in motion, while our definitions are always static, trying to put God in a box, saying God is this or that. But for Job God is a whirlwind. "And from the heart of the tempest Yahweh gave Job his answer." His answer is like a hundred questions!

The first question is, "Who is this obscuring my designs with his empty-headed words?" We might be tempted to say, "God, you're not being nice to Job. He deserves better."

Implicitly God is saying, "I'm going to tell you who I am and I'm going to tell you that I'm on your side. And I'm going to give you the power to believe that. Brace yourself, Job. Now it is my turn to ask questions and yours to inform me" (verse 3).

"You've had thirty-seven chapters of questions," God goes on, "now I'm going to give you mine. And I'm only going to have two chapters."

All God's questions

First, Yahweh describes the earth. This reverses the order of Genesis, which begins with the light, then moves on to the sea, then to the earth. Here, we have the earth and then the sea and then the light. Yahweh describes the earth as a building — wonderful poetry once again.

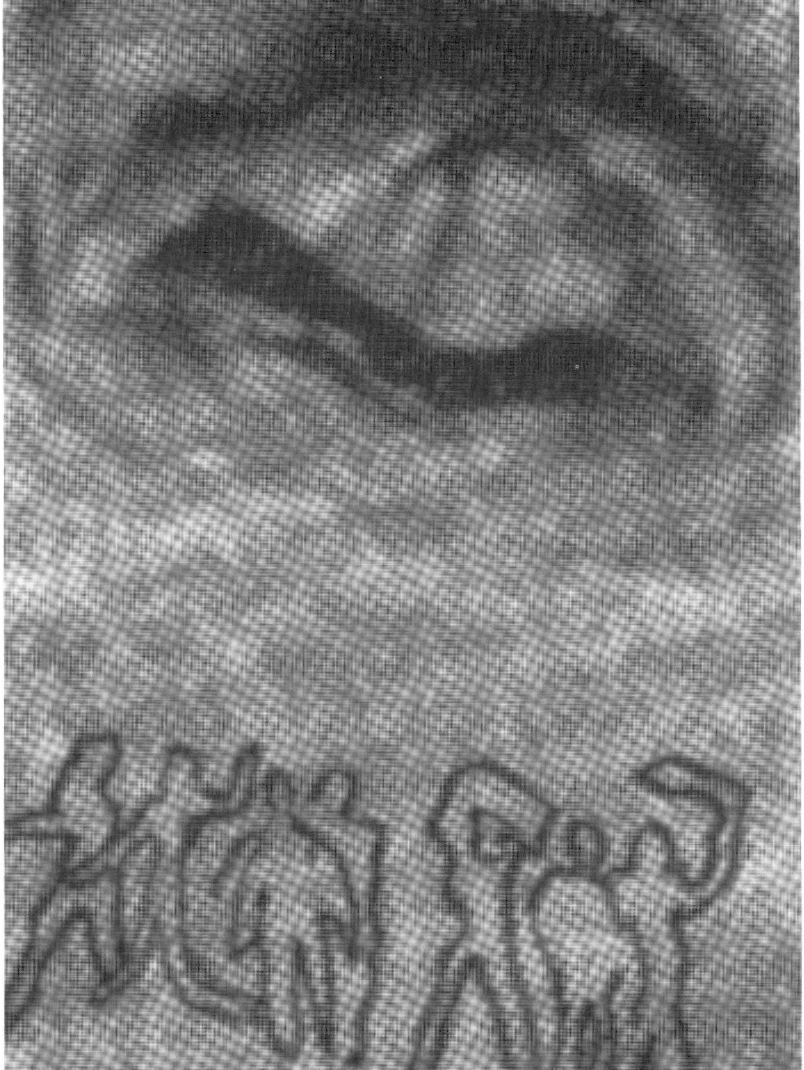

"Where were you when I laid the earth's foundations? Tell me, since you are so well informed. Who decided the dimensions of it, do you know? Or who stretched the measuring line across it? What supports its pillars at their bases? Who laid its cornerstone? When all the stars of the morning were singing with joy, and all the heavenly beings in chorus were chanting praise?" (38:4–7).

Where were you, Job? It is a question to daunt anyone, high or low.

Then the sea. The great and horrible sea is described as a baby — imagery only a poet would dare to use. "Who pent up the sea behind closed doors when it leaped tumultuous out of the womb, when I wrapped it in a robe of mist and made black clouds its swaddling bands; when I marked the bounds it was not to cross and made it fast with a bolted gate? 'Come thus far,' I said, 'and no farther: Here your proud waves shall break'" (38:8–11).

So the sea is as a little child created by God. "It looks so powerful to you," he is saying, but to me it's only a child.

And then he describes light. Job, "have you ever in your life given orders to the morning, or sent the dawn to its post, telling it to grasp the earth by its edges and shake the wicked out of it, when it changes the earth to sealing clay . . . stealing the light from wicked men and breaking the arm raised to strike?" (38:12–15).

In verses 16 to 23 God speaks of sources and origins. "Have you journeyed all the way to the sources of the sea? . . . Have you been shown the gates of death, or met the janitors of Shadowland? Have you an inkling of the extent of the earth? Tell me all about it if you have! Which is the way to the home of the light, and where does darkness live? You could then show them the way to their proper places. . . . Have you ever visited the place where the snow is kept, or seen where the hail is stored up, which I keep for times of stress, for days of battle and war?"

Next God wants to know whether Job, if he were in charge of the world, would know how to run it. Would he know how to keep the equipment going? If he were janitor of the world, would he know which buttons to push? Well, I do, God says.

"Who carves a channel for the downpour, and hacks a way for the rolling thunder?...Has the rain a father? Who begets the dewdrops? What womb brings forth the ice, and gives birth to the frost of heaven? Can you fasten the harness of the Pleides, or untie Orion's bands?...Can you guide the morning star season by season?...Have you grasped the celestial laws?" (38:25–32).

Yahweh pushes harder, revealing God as both awesome and alluring, both fascinating and fearsome. "Can your voice carry as far as the clouds, and make the pent-up waters do your bidding? Will lightning flashes come at your command, and answer, 'Here we are'?...Who gave the ibis wisdom and endowed the cock with foreknowledge?" (38:34–36).

God boasts about the animals

As we see, God begins to describe a number of animals and birds. He emphasizes his loving care for each of these, each of which he has created. God says, in effect, that Job could never have imagined such animals or designed them or provided for them. Many of us probably share this feeling when confronted with the many corny-looking animals in existence. "Why would God create something that looks like a peacock?" we ask. Or a giraffe? Why create so many wondrous-looking animals? God must have a sense of humor.

It seems the person who wrote these chapters had a similar human reaction. The author picks a number of different animals and of each one God seems to say, "I did that just because I enjoy it. I love this beauty. I love this light. I love lions and goats. I know how many months it takes them to carry their young. I know the exact time they give birth. They crouch to drop their young. They let their burdens fall on the open desert. My eyes are watching them all." It's a feast of nonnecessity, God reveling in the lovely gratuity of it all.

The image projected is of a profuse and providential God. It is an intimation of what Jesus will say in the New Testament, that he knows even when a sparrow falls. "Who gave the wild donkey his freedom?...I have given him the desert as a home....Is the wild ox willing to serve you?...Can the wing of the ostrich be compared with the plumage of the stork or falcon?" (39:5–13). The descriptions are specific and magnificent, an animal lover describing the work of an animal-lover God.

"Are you the one who makes the horse so brave?...Do you make him leap like a grasshopper?...He laughs at fear. ...On his back the quiver rattles, the flashing spear and javelin, at each trumpet blast he shouts 'Hurrah!' He scents the battle from afar, hearing the thundering of chiefs, the shouting" (39:19–25).

The section adds nothing new to what Job's friends have already said about God's wonder. They all said God is in charge, God loves creation. The difference is that in this chapter *God* is saying it. Therefore we are to believe it. The language is moving from a juridical horizon of should's and ought's to a vast horizon formed by the gratuity of God's love. Space is opening up for both God and Job, and for a new relationship. The conversation moves into an entirely different framework because love is so much broader and deeper than any theology of retribution.

God is telling us that he is excited about life in all its forms. He revels in life. No matter how many times we destroy it, no matter how many people we kill, God keeps creating more life. Whatever else our theologies might say or deny, we cannot deny that God is a lover of life (see Wisd. 11:24–27). So his people, if they are truly his people, will always love and protect life in all its myriad forms.

One of the scary, horrible aspects of the world today is

that we have learned so well to make friends with death and are so comfortable with killing people and destroying things; that we take this planet, with all its life, so lightly. Deep down we know such destructiveness is the antithesis of the God described in this book.

God, for some inscrutable reason, shows himself in all kinds of created beauty. The height of this beauty is our own human nature. Therefore we must, at all costs, protect the treasure that is human life and let no nation's laws take it away. But these verses give a high priority to animal life as well. Western Christians would do well to reflect on the implications. When any segment of the "great chain of being" is disrespected, the entire chain is weakened and the sacred is lost.

In chapter 40 Yahweh turns to Job and says, "Is Shaddai's opponent willing to give in? Has God's critic thought up an answer?" And we can just imagine Job's mind racing in reaction: "Oh, no, no, I'm just glad you're taking me seriously. I know it's not answering anything, but it's you, and I don't care what you say as long as we are talking. You are giving me *you* and that's all I want!"

Acceptance

"My words have been frivolous," he says. "What can I reply? I had better lay my finger on my lips. I have spoken once... I will not speak again" (40:3–5). I don't believe Job is shamed by God as much as he just wants to hear God keep talking. So the Lord continues, still speaking, we are reminded, "out of the tempest."

"Brace yourself as a fighter," God goes on in verse 7 (he repeats this fighter metaphor, as if to endorse Job's fighting spirit). "This is the kind of person I can wrestle with," he seems to be saying, "those who are not afraid to fight with me. Those who are not afraid to get in and be brother, son, lifegiver, lover, even — in hard times — enemy to me. Those who care enough to fight me are the ones I can probably make into the best friends."

The importance of otherness

There has been much upset or at least disappointment with the God of the Book of Job, who merely speaks from "a whirlwind" and does not really answer any of Job's rightful questions. Some think that God is merely pulling the old authority ploy or even saying, "It's none of your business." There seems to be no objective response to Job's legitimate and painful questions. Even if Job appears to be content in the story, we are seldom content as readers. For us the subjective problems of evil, unjust suffering, and hidden God remain personal dilemmas, and sometimes agonizing ones. We want some objective response from God.

I want to try to say something that I believe is very important in every age, but surely in this postmodern age that has thrown out all hope of any objective answers for anything. I believe that the opposite of subjectivity is not objectivity but *otherness*. That probably sounds pretty abstract and philosophical, but it is crucial to appreciating what God is doing for Job in this narrative. God makes no attempt to respond to each concern point by point because it will not really satisfy anyway.

I have learned painfully that every attempt to respond to an underlying "ideology of resentment" usually only deepens the resentment. People seem actually disappointed that you have defused their underlying alienation with a logical response, and they invariably pick at something else because the heart and soul are unsatisfied.

Jesus himself either remains silent before his antagonists or *never* answers their hostile questions. Check it out in the Gospels. He never responds directly but tries to aim the dialogue in another direction that will hopefully reframe the question.

God seems to be a great dodger of most human questions. The good-willed will always allow this because they want truth and relationship above all else. The ill-willed will only string out the debate into impossible scenarios. As we all say, "You never win." (I know this for a fact from twenty-five years of audience response. The first sentence out of a respondent's mouth usually gives away the stance, and it is very hard to change if they have already hardened their heart against you.)

It is an openness to the other — as other — that frees us for creativity and originality in our response: the other who is somehow outside my social system or the Absolute Other who gives me a reference point that relativizes all of my own. It is always an encounter with *otherness* that changes me. If I am not open to beyond-me, I'm in trouble. Without the other, we are trapped inside a perpetual hall of mirrors that only validates and deepens my existing worldviews.

One could say that the central theme of the biblical revelation is to call people to encounters with otherness: the alien, the sinner, the Samaritan, the Gentile, the hidden and denied self, angels unaware. And all of these perhaps, in preparation and training for hopeful meetings with true transcendence, the Absolute Other. We need practice in moving outside of our comfort zones. It is never a natural response.

The God who speaks to Job out of the whirlwind is not an answer giver or a problem solver. God does more than that. God frees Job and every believer from their hall of mirrors, their prison of self where they cannot see or understand. God gives us a place to stand "from which we can move the world," like Archimedes' leverage.

After struggling with an aphorism from the saints for many years, I think I finally understand what they were saying: "There is no true knowledge without faith." The faith encounter with a transcendent reference point is the only thing that will put everything else into proper perspective. Without faith, all knowledge is a Heraclitean river, mere information used for pragmatic purposes of self and often against one another. The postmoderns are actually right if they are speaking to a secular world. Everything is subjective, passing, and in flux.

The fruit of the biblical revelation depends more than anything else *on having a Lord.* (Even our rejection of the word under the guise of sexist connotations reveals the extent of our fear, autonomy, and rebellion against any outer superiority.) "Having a Lord," in whatever phraseology we care to use, implies that another is my teacher and I am the taught, another is in control and I am not, another is the reference point and I am the disposable one.

As affronting as this is to contemporary sensibilities, it is simply metaphysical truth and therefore the fullest kind of freedom. If these chapters are not teaching such liberating lordship, I am not sure if they are saying anything.

Allowing God to be our Lord is not something we can do as easily as believing this, doing that, attending this, or avoiding that. It is always a process of a lifetime, a movement toward union that will always feel like a loss of self-importance and autonomy. The private ego will resist and rationalize in every way that it can. My experience is that, apart from suffering, failure, humiliation, and pain, none of us will naturally let go of our self-sufficiency. We will think that our story is just about *us.* It isn't.

Such selfish autonomy is not just a matter of pride in competition with God; rather it is a lie. The private and cut-off image of self has no foundation in any kind of reality. It is an illusion, and all religion is trying to help us overcome this illusion by regrafting *(re-ligio)* us to the vine where we are, in fact, already grafted. It is a matter of "doing the truth" in every aspect of our life. "Remain in me as I remain in you...for cut off from me you can do nothing" (John 15:4–5).

This entire journey of Job can best be seen as the painful path of the soul: the "pruning" of the branch of its pretense of autonomy and all the burden that goes with it — self-validation and self-criticism. Freedom is when you know that neither of them matters. My significance comes from who-I-am-in-God, who-I-am-as-part-of-a-much-larger-whole. I am somehow a representative of God; and God is carrying me, both the good and the bad parts. There seem to be only two ways that we know this experientially: *prayer and suffering.* I think that is perhaps the central message of the whole Bible, but surely the message of the Book of Job.

Hippos — and the dinosaur story

In the midst of these magnificent speeches, for some unexplainable reason, we find thrown in a description of a hippopotamus ("behemoth"). And a whole chapter of description of a crocodile ("leviathan") (40:15–41:26). Why? And why here?

This is my conjecture. The hippopotamus and crocodile are first of all uncontrollable, naturally meaningless animals. They are purposeless — and ugly. Why would God create something like these? They are images of a power that is chaotic, random, and seemingly unnecessary. They are the wild cards — or even the jokers — in a seemingly coherent universe.

It appears that the author is offering the hippopotamus and crocodile as images of that wild and free part of God that we can't control or understand. Just as we marvel and are puzzled at the hippopotamus and crocodile, God will always be to us a similar marvel and mystery. And we would be unwise to try to take the marvel and mystery away. It's no accident that the trickster or clown figure has appeared in almost all world literature to make way for this divine whimsy.

It seems a strange technique to put these animals in here, but then I realize how often over the years I have told my dinosaur story. (All right, I'll tell it again!) The point is not theological or anything so profound, but it does place things in a radically new perspective.

Some years ago, I was in New York with another member of the community, and we went to the American Museum of Natural History and we saw the dinosaurs. We were standing there in wonder and awe, and I turned to Michael and asked how long ago did those dinosaurs live on earth. And he said, "Oh, about 200 million years."

We stood there a while longer in wonder and awe. Two hundred million years ago! I asked him, "How long were they on the earth?" He said, "I think they were on the earth 150 million years." (Both wrong, I have since discovered!)

We stood there again in wonder and awe. One hundred and fifty million years, these guys were crawling around the earth. And I turned to him somewhat facetiously and said, "Michael, what did they do for 150 million years?" And he said, "They ate grass."

People always laugh at that, I don't know why. Then I said to Michael, "They were on the earth for 150 million years and just eating grass? What was God doing all that time?" And he said, "Well, I guess he was watching them eat grass."

Someone told me that's the most profound theological story I've ever told. So if I can talk about the dinosaur, Job can talk about the hippopotamus and the crocodile. It seems to suggest that there is an illogical/chaotic part to this world that leaves us out of full control — no matter how smart or holy we are. God is not just a clockmaker or creator of perfect order. God is also trickster, exception, foil, and surprise. God is personal and not just predictable force.

Small fry in the galaxies

Carl Sagan, in one segment of his astronomy series "Cosmos," describes the Milky Way. He shows a giant photograph of the Milky Way, and he says, "You probably imagine we're right in the center. No, we're way out here in the corner. And what we call the sun is just one little sun among billions of suns in this one galaxy, and then there are billions of galaxies." The very thought of that should do something to us, help us put ourselves in perspective.

And I'm standing here talking about God? I'm presuming to understand with this little head? It's inconceivable. We're one little planet in one galaxy in the midst of billions of galaxies, and we dare to presume to understand what's going on. And then we get righteous about our theologies. I'm saved if I do this. I'm saved if I do that. If you don't get dipped totally in the water, you're not saved. If you don't call God by the right name, he won't like you. It's hard to believe people can be that lost in their own little world and their own private importance. God does not allow Job to make that mistake.

Job's personal problem is, in one sense, completely ignored. Nothing is said about guilt, nothing is said about innocence, or about the meaning of suffering. And that was supposed to be the whole meaning of this book, wasn't it? The meaning of suffering. God gives no answer. God *is* Job's integrity.

Job therefore no longer has to prove his own integrity. He doesn't need to win it. He doesn't need to possess it. That is his freedom. Not to need to win. Not to need to prove that you're right. Not to need to fix anything.

Job is an image of true enlightenment. He does not possess God as a product or an attainment, but God possesses him. He is regrafted to the vine that he already is. The ontological question, which is the essential religious question, is answered.

In chapter 42 we find the answer Job finally gave back to Yahweh. It is the second climax of the book. "I know that you are all-powerful. What you conceive, you can perform. I am the man who obscured your designs with my empty-headed words. I have been holding forth on matters I cannot understand, on marvels beyond me and my knowledge. I knew you then only by hearsay; but now, having seen you with my own eyes, I retract all I have said, and in dust and ashes I repent" (42:1–6). None of his questions are answered, but he has *seen!* The question of *being,* who-he-is, *has* been answered, and that answers all the other questions.

Job finally feeling good

At last Job's desire is fulfilled — to see with his own eyes and not "by hearsay." To see and be seen. That's all any of us desire. For some eyes to go through us and understand. For someone to see us naked as God saw Adam, and not call us ugly. To see us naked and not name us foolish. We desire to be seen all the way through. "Who told you that you were naked?" said God to Adam in the garden (Gen. 3:11).

Job has been seen and acknowledged, so he no longer needs answers: "I retract all that I have said, God, and in dust and ashes I repent." It is not a groveling in the dirt; it's not a self-hatred. It's a life-giving new spaciousness. In fact, some translators insist that it is best said, "I repudiate the dust-and-ashes mentality." In other words, I have no need to blame or to defend.

His estrangement has been taken away. He can say, in effect, "It doesn't matter. You're looking at me and I'm looking at you." Union has been reestablished. He might paraphrase Paul and say, "Once we saw a dim reflection in a mirror, but now we see one another face to face" (1 Cor. 13:12). And that makes all the difference.

It becomes evident at this point that the hero of this book is Job, not God. And God *allows* Job to be the hero. In a certain sense, after Job's speeches, God's speech is beautiful poetry, but it's anticlimactic. God does put the issue in a new perspective, but God is not the hero of this drama. Job is. And for that reason this book lays claim to being the most magnificent piece of religious drama ever written. Because it's doing exactly what God is doing in history.

God loves us so perfectly, he lets us be the heroes. God lets us, like Israel ("strong against God"), wrestle with the angel of Yahweh, lets us struggle with God *and win* (Gen. 32:28). So to us goes the glory precisely when we give God the glory. When we try to let go and give our life to God, God gives it back to us.

Should we be surprised? That's what love does. That's the only thing you can get excited about when you're in love — giving your life to the other and seeing enjoyment in the other. That's the union toward which God is calling us. The lover delighting in the beloved and the beloved delighting in the lover.

The epilogue at the end probably goes back to the original story. Job finally gets his "justice." God has become his witness, his just judge, and his defender. "When Yahweh had said all this to Job, he turned to Eliphaz of Teman. "I burn with anger against you and your friends," he says, "for not speaking truthfully about me as my servant Job has done" (42:7). God is angry with what most would call correct and orthodox theology. Quite amazing and rather irresponsible on God's part.

Truth is more a person than an idea

The three stooges who pretended to be his friends get a theological kick in the behind. All their beautiful arguments about God were false according to God's own word. They did not understand communion, such as the communion Job and God had. They talked from outside that union. Therefore, what they spoke, even though theologically correct, was personally, subjectively wrong.

"So now, find seven bullocks and seven rams, and take them back with you to my servant, Job, and offer a holocaust for yourselves, while Job, my servant, offers prayers for you" (42:8). Job is now justified before God and becomes an intercessor for his brothers. "I will listen to him with favor [we can practically hear Job sighing with relief at the notion that God is listening to him] and excuse your folly in not speaking of me properly as my servant Job has done" (42:9).

Eliphaz, Bildad, and Zophar "went away to do as Yahweh had ordered, and Yahweh listened to Job with favor. Yahweh restored Job's fortunes, because he had prayed for his friends" (42:9–10). His redemption is not complete until he prays for those who caused him such pain.

Even this early in the history of salvation it was necessary for Job to forgive his friends — to extend that communion that he had experienced with God to the three who had given him such a bad time. The height of spirituality is never anything but the *imitatio Dei,* the imitation of God.

More than that, Yahweh gave Job double what he had before. It was a way of saying, "If you thought I loved you before, now I love you double." (Or is it Job's capacity that has doubled?) And all of his brothers and sisters and friends from former times came to see him and sat down at table with him (42:11). The image of the table signifies communion with all that he thought he lost.

"Yahweh blessed Job's new fortune even more than his first. He came to own 14,000 sheep, 6,000 camels, 1,000 yoke of oxen, and 1,000 she-donkeys. He had seven sons and three daughters. His first daughter he called Turtledove and the second Cassia and the third Mascara" (42:12–14). Don't ask me why.

"Throughout the land there were no women as beautiful as the daughters of Job [it gets almost playful here, as if the author is relieved to stop talking about dire deeds and serious issues and get back to the comfortable trivia of daily life]. Their father gave them inheritance rights like their brothers" (42:15). Job was, therefore, the first feminist, for this was not the practice of the day.

"After his trials, Job lived on until he was 140 years old, and saw his children and his children's children up to the fourth generation. Then Job died, an old man and full of days."

Coda

One way to bring all this into the twentieth century is with a Peanuts cartoon from the 1970s. Charlie Brown is standing on the pitcher's mound. He says, "Boy, it sure has been bad lately." Little Linus comes up to him and says: "Don't criticize the world, Charlie Brown. Where were you when he laid the foundations of the earth? Who laid its cornerstone when its morning stars sang together? Who shut in the sea with doors when it burst forth from the womb? Charlie Brown, have you entered the storehouse of the snow? Who can number the clouds by wisdom? Who can tilt the waterskins of the heavens [as he holds his pitcher's mitt up to the sky]? Is the wild ox willing to serve you? Do you give the horse his might? Is it by your wisdom that the hawk soars and spreads his wings to the South?"

And Charlie just stands there on the pitcher's mound, wondering, "Do I deserve all this?"

"Don't criticize the world, Charlie Brown," Linus repeats as he walks away. Then Charlie shouts after him: "How would it be if I just yelled at the umpire?"

Chapter 9

Out of the Shadow of God's Light

THE PROBLEM OF EVIL is one of the greatest dilemmas with which humans are asked to come to grips. It's much easier to discuss it theologically than to cope with it in real life. But sooner or later we all meet the little boy dying of leukemia, or the out-of-work father of five whose wife is disabled. We are prompted to say, "Where is God?"

We meet the saintly old man or woman, maybe suffering several diseases, alone and lonely, whose family no longer exists or no longer cares. Confronted with such sufferings, we don't even know how to pray. We say, if we're honest like Job, "Where is God?"

Then there is collective evil. Powerful nations prepare to destroy competing nations in the name of security. We see corporate corruption and international greed. There is a collective evil out there bigger than any of us, and we don't know how our lives can deal with it. We see most of the world without justice, without enough food, without enough medical care, without basic human rights.

I know of people unjustly imprisoned here at the jail. Try to imagine how you would feel to be locked up unjustly just for one day. This is the only life they've got, and it's being taken away from them. The problem of evil gets real when we remove it from theological abstraction and even from the historical person of Job thousands of years ago and confront it in real life.

We pray in the Our Father that the Lord will not lead us to

this kind of test, because none of us is sure we could bear it. The grace to bear it is never given until the moment arrives, and then we have to pray. My hope is that this book is doing some of our homework ahead of time, which was the historic meaning of "initiation."

Three options on the evil issue

The Book of Job suggests three solutions to the problem of evil. The first is that God is not all-powerful. The second is that God is not good or just. The third is that humanity is the cause of evil.

The friends of Job select the third option. They say, in essence, that human nature is bad. Job himself chooses the second option, that God is not just. Because I know I'm good, he bravely argues, it must be God.

If I had to choose between the three, I'd draw closest to the first. Our definition of God as all-powerful and always in charge is not adequate. We have assumed in a common-sense way that God is all-powerful, sovereign, everywhere in control. That is not an adequate explanation. I believe that somehow power can be seen as slipping from God's hands. The Lord is not always Lord, it seems. God, in giving us the gift of freedom, seems to have given up at least some omnipotence.

As long as Job is healthy and wealthy, we can keep all three options open. The system breaks down only when suffering, particularly unjust suffering, intrudes into the story. So Job begins to struggle with the goodness of God, with the power of God, and with his own goodness or sinfulness. Struggle seems to be the only way to create a *disinterested love* in us. Remember Satan's first challenge to God, "But Job is not God-fearing for nothing, is he?" (1:9). It's the "for nothing" that God is expanding in Job—and in us.

Somehow the system has to fall apart. Then we begin our wrestling match with God. We begin to deal with the problem of imperfection, of living in a limited, imperfect world. Before this, we demand perfection of the world and expect it of ourselves. This demanding attitude makes love, especially unconditional love, next to impossible. Why are we so presumptuous as to think we should be perfect? Why do we find it so hard to love imperfect things? We seem to believe that only perfect things are worthy of our love.

Jesus addresses the problem in Matthew 13:12–30. This is one of the most important parables in the New Testament, although also one of the most neglected in the Christian tradition.

Go easy on the weeds

Genesis told us that God created the world good. Yet that is not always our experience. Part of the problem is that we define good as ordered and harmonious. I think, rather, that good refers to what is capable of being made ordered and harmonious. Bringing about that ordering and harmony is precisely the task God gives to human nature.

So, in Matthew 13:24 Jesus says, "The kingdom of heaven may be compared to a man who sowed good seed in his field. But then, while everybody was asleep, his enemy came, sowed 'darnel' [weeds that grow in cultivated fields] all among the wheat, and made off."

In a simplistic way we think of the enemy as Satan. Yes, but it's also the world and the flesh. It's the combination of all the lies of culture, the lies of history, family, and our own brokenness, lies that we tell ourselves and one another for the sake of some kind of minimal survival. We ourselves sow weeds among the wheat, lies among the truth.

However, "when the new wheat sprouted and then ripened, the darnel appeared as well. The owner's servants went to him and said, 'Sir, was it not good seed that you sowed in your field? If so, where does the darnel come from?' " (Matt. 13:27).

And that is always our question. Where do the weeds come from? We try to be good. We think we're Christian. Yet we have the most horrible thoughts. And we do things we do not understand. We hurt the very people we do not want to hurt. We know our own individual lives have brought their share of evil into this world. We feel guilty about that and we're sorry.

Why, as Paul says in Romans 7:15, "do I do the very things I don't want to do?" All of us have struggled with that at some point. In this parable we see that Jesus understands our struggle and inconsistency. "Some enemy has done this," the owner answered. Immediately we want to blame it on someone else.

So the servants asked, "Do you want us to go and weed it out?" And Jesus gives a most extraordinary answer, a very different one from what most moralists and confessors have given us. Jesus says, "No, because when you weed out the weeds you might pull up the wheat with it."

That's nothing like any good Catholic boy or girl was ever taught. Yet, Jesus said this. We haven't dealt with much that Jesus said. His life was so superior to ours that the best history has been able to do is grow a year each century in our ability to deal with Jesus. That makes the church about twenty years old, morally speaking. We're just growing up. We're just beginning to ask adult questions of the Gospel. For the most part we've been asking childish questions, or adolescent questions. But now we're twenty. And we're beginning to admit that Jesus said some things that, for some reason, we ignored. Children are not able to deal with some things, especially subtlety or paradox.

Jesus says, *"Let them both grow until the harvest"* (Matt. 13:30). In the harvest "I'll say to the reapers, 'Separate the weeds and the wheat.' " We are unwilling, it seems, to leave any work for the reapers.

We have spent most of our lives trying to do the job of separation ourselves, trying to figure out who the good guys are and who the bad guys are. It's a waste of time, Jesus land. 11But stretch out your hand now, and touch all that he has, and he will curse you to your face." 12T[illegible]RD said to Satan,[d] "Very well, [illegible] has is in your power; only d[illegible]h out your hand against him!" S[illegible]an[d] went out from the presence of [illegible]RD.

13 One day when hi[illegible]augh-ters were eating and [illegible] in the eldest brother's h[illegible]enger came to Job and [illegible] were plowing and [illegible]onk[illegible]ding beside them [illegible]nd th[illegible]ans [illegible] on them and [illegible] them [illegible]nd kil[illegible] the servants [illegible] the e[illegible]e sw[illegible]d; I alone [illegible]e escaped [illegible]." 16While he wa[illegible]ill speaki[illegible]er cam[illegible]nd said, "The fire of [illegible] from [illegible]n and burned up [illegible] and th[illegible]er-vants, and cons[illegible]th[illegible] alone have escaped to tell [illegible] 17W[illegible] he was still speaking, an[illegible] came [illegible] said, "The Chaldeans fo[illegible] three c[illegible]mns, made a raid on the [illegible]ls and car[illegible]em off, and killed th[illegible]vants with [illegible]ge of the sword; I [illegible]ne have escape[illegible]ell you." 18Wh[illegible]e was still speakin[illegible] other came [illegible] said, "Your sons [illegible] daughters [illegible]ating and drinking [illegible]ne in their el[illegible]rother's house, 19an[illegible] sud-denly [illegible]eat wind came across the desert, struck the four corners of the

God with wrong-doing.

2 One day the heavenly beings[c] came to present them[illegible]es before the LORD, and Satan[d] als[illegible]mong them to present himself b[illegible] LORD. 2The LORD said to Satan [illegible]re have you come from?" Satan[e] an[illegible]ed the LORD, "From going to and f[illegible]e earth, and from walking up a[illegible]it." 3The LORD said to Sat[illegible] consid-ered my servant [illegible] one like him on the ear[illegible]d upright man who fe[illegible]n [illegible]way from evil. H[illegible] his [illegible]grity, al-thor[illegible]e ag[illegible] him, to d[illegible]ason. [illegible]hen Sa-t[illegible]D, "Ski[illegible] skin! [illegible] they will [illegible] to [illegible]ut stretch ou[illegible]uch his bone an[illegible] will curse you to your fac[illegible] 6The [illegible]d to Satan,[d] "Very well, he is i[illegible]r; only spare his life."

7 S[illegible]an[illegible]nt out from the pres-ence o[illegible]ORD, [illegible]nd inflicted loathsome sores [illegible]b fro[illegible]he sole of his foot to the c[illegible]n of his [illegible]ad. 8Job[g] took a pot-sher[illegible]th which to scrape himself, and sat [illegible]ng the ashes.

[illegible]n his wife said to him, "Do you persist in your integrity? Curse[h] God, and die." 10But he said to her, "You speak as any foolish woman would seems to say: "Be children of your Father in heaven, who causes the sun to rise on the bad and the good, and the rain to fall on the just and the unjust" (Matt. 5:45).

I'm certain of one thing at this point in my life: that a great many things I thought were weeds when I first started my journey have turned out to be my wheat. So many things I was sure were my greatest virtues — my best wheat — have turned out to be my demons and weeds. And if I had pulled them out too quickly, as my early formation directors encouraged me to do, I would have lost some of my greatest gifts. Many have been attacking the enemy that wasn't the enemy.

Conversely, much that I thought was my wheat, my true gifts, have turned out to be the source of my greatest and most denied faults. Only time and suffering sorted them out a bit. Thus Jesus courageously says, "Let them both grow together until the harvest." Quite amazing and quite untraditional teaching. Jesus does not see religion as the enforcement of law and order in the world, but much more as the school of the soul, the training ground for union.

The only way the enemy succeeds is by disguising himself. "The angels of darkness must disguise themselves as angels of light" (2 Cor. 11:14). Most of us do not possess much discernment about true good and true evil unless we are taught by the Spirit (1 Cor. 12:10). As Paul insists repeatedly, the law is not the same as the spirit (Rom. 4:14, Gal. 22:15–21). The law gives information at best. The spirit gives wisdom and strength to understand the true purpose and intention of the law.

Sins we turned a blind eye on

For centuries we have put up with direct disobedience to Jesus in the church and have been incapable of recognizing it as sin. Indeed we have even promoted people in the church for being agents of some of these evils. Ambition, for example; greed, power, vanity, and idolatry are commonly lived by the clergy and laity — without our feeling the need to rationalize, or blush. These are not subject to legislation, like sexual acts, but only to discernment and prayer.

We in the priesthood were repeatedly warned about going to bed with women — which, I guess, if we took a vow of celibacy, we should be — but why did no one warn us about going to bed with ambition? Or going to bed with power? Or going to bed with money? For some reason we didn't recognize those demons. We do not see the air that we breathe.

That is a lack of discernment. It has been a cancer inside the church, keeping it from recognizing the poor Christ. And the power of Christ. And the love of Christ. We have always railed against sins which were specific, measurable, and shame-based instead of the much more subtle demons which suffocate and destroy the power of the Gospel in God's people. Moral teaching seems to be a matter of control and cultural sanction, much more than the teaching and emphasis of Jesus.

The key moral question is not, "How can we get rid of evil?" but rather, "How can we use evil for good?" How can we learn discernment so that we can say, yes, this is weed and that is wheat, but they must both grow together to create life? That is the great moral question. That is the true challenge for spiritual guides — how to put together darkness and light. How else do you explain the supreme effectiveness of the murder of Jesus?

Now Jesus used the prepsychological language of darkness and light. Today, we are so psychologically attuned that if we merely use spiritual language, such as darkness and light, we may not be understood. It tends to be mystified and often evaporates into greeting card language.

The *language* I find most helpful for the spiritual tasks of today (the *concepts* are already clear in Jesus) has been given us by Carl Jung. He described that state of disguised darkness within us as the "shadow" self.

The shadow, of itself, is not evil. But when evil happens in our lives, it's often when we are unaware of our own shadow. The greatest danger is to see no evil in ourselves. Or to pretend that, because we went to confession, sin no longer has a hold over us.

The shadow is a part of the self we fear. We pretend, therefore, that it isn't there. The shadow is the unacceptable self. Who made it unacceptable? Mom, Dad, the pastor — everyone who passed on to us some of their unlived life, their control needs, angers, hang-ups. Sometimes these have little to do with actual moral evil and have more to do with our parents' and pastors' cultural fears.

The shadow is that part of the self that we're afraid to live and even afraid to recognize or afraid to feel. Those thoughts we're afraid to imagine. And we think that because we refuse to acknowledge them, they are gone. That's our big mistake. Because what we repress or shove into our unconscious is exactly what mostly controls us. Jesus has clearly taught this in commanding the love of the enemy and his harsh admonition, "Hypocrite! Take the plank out of your own eye first, and then you will see clearly enough to take the splinter out of another's" (Matt. 7:5).

It is particularly insidious because it comes to us from a camouflaged and disguised position, from a place where we have no creative control over it. And we don't therefore know why we are depressed every third day, why we're irritable and threatened. I think the reason fear has gained such power in the West is because fear has been denied. And the people who are going to be most controlled by their fears are the ones who don't admit them and deal with them. Similarly with anger, hatred, and all the rest.

Humor is of the essence

One of the symptoms of a large and repressed shadow world is the lack of a sense of humor. People who can't laugh or can't enjoy, especially those who can't laugh at themselves, are in trouble. This is one of the best rules of thumb in the spiritual life: If we can't let others poke fun at us, we probably have a large, denied shadow. Everything inside becomes a sacred cow. We say to people, "Don't touch!" because we ourselves are afraid to touch it.

People with a large and repressed shadow world usually will be stern and moralistic. They walk through life shaking the finger. We all, at some time, had a teacher like that. For such people, everything under heaven has a moral judgment attached to it. They also tend to be incapable of enjoyment. Life is to be judged in terms of good and bad, better and worse, mortal and venial, hell and purgatory. They can't let things be or let life happen without a smothering value judgment.

When we spend all our energy keeping that unacceptable self denied, there's no energy left for humor or fun. People who have a large shadow world tend to be fearful: Aimless anxiety is one of the main ways the shadow shows itself. They often tend to be angry, too. They're forever looking for a projection screen for their anger when, in fact, they're really angry at themselves or at life in general.

People out of touch with their shadow self tend to be needlessly guilty. We used to call that scrupulosity. I guess we still do, but we don't seem to produce as many scrupulous folk. It used to be a disease almost endemic to Catholicism. People were unnecessarily guilty because they had this assumption that they had to be perfect to please God. That's the root of the problem, and where we have to face it. We think — wrongly — that God can only love perfect things. What a tiny and weak God that would be.

Only when we pretend the shadow is not there does it have an evil effect on us and on the world. When we pretend we're not angry, that's when we're victims of our anger. There are a lot of enraged people going around pretending they're not angry. Everybody can see it except themselves.

As a spiritual director and confessor I see the shadow

constantly. And I am so grateful that something like the sacrament of reconciliation has been maintained. If it did not exist, we would have to invent it. Maybe that's why therapists are doing so well. People who are not in touch with their shadow self will, as certainly as tomorrow's dawn, project it onto other people or events. Instead of recognizing it within ourselves we hate it "over there." The Hebrews creatively constructed a ritual for this, the scapegoat that was sent out into the desert bearing their sins (Lev. 16:20–22).

We call it projection. The sin and brokenness and hatefulness of ourselves that we can't accept in ourselves, we hate in other people. And as long as we don't recognize and forgive faults in ourselves, we'll find an individual or group to project them onto. The scapegoat mechanism is the rationalization for most of the violence in the world; indeed it even sacralizes much of that violence.

The mote is in my eye, Mate

So we get back to what Teresa of Avila began with in the first room of the "interior castle." We have to know ourselves. We shouldn't talk about a spiritual life, or about knowing God, until we know ourselves. And people who don't know themselves are, for the most part, incapable of knowing God. There is no constituted self to meet another self, much less *the* Self.

Our concept of God will largely be a projection of our own unfulfilled egotism, our unknown self and our desire for what we think God should be rather than what God really is. Such people never meet God; they simply meet who they want God to be, what they need God to be each moment. When God turns out not to match their expectations, they consciously or indirectly reject the search for God.

If there is a revolution in spirituality today, it is a returning to the true sense of what Jesus initially taught: that we come to God through our imperfection, through our wounds, in fact. Isn't that exactly the message of the crucified one? When we can live with him, can accept his humble, broken state, and even rejoice in it, then we're free. Then we are truly poor men and women, with nothing to protect, with no illusions to maintain before ourselves or other people. There's no other freedom to match that. Or no love!

Then we are free to walk through this world and enjoy its goodness before we need to balk at its badness. We're free to accept what is in front of us without needing to change it or control it. Always remember that the best ally of God is *what is.* Not what should be, what could be, what needs be, but what is. "Isness" will lead us to perfect love.

All things are partially light and partially darkness — all things, including the pope, the church, our bishop, and ourselves. The problem is not out there. The problem isn't your church or the fact that your husband isn't perfect. You've got to begin, as Jesus always said, with yourself." We have met the primary enemy — and it is *us.* What a relief when we can let go of the need to explain and fix others.

Imperfection is good enough

The reason I can speak with authority on this is that, after fifty years, I'm still fighting it. I was raised to try to be perfect. I always wanted to be perfect and was sure God would not love me if I were not perfect. I was equally sure no one else would love me if I were not perfect. So I drove myself. I didn't want to be just like everyone else. I had to leave Kansas and run off to Cincinnati and put this Franciscan robe on. This would make me perfect. This would make God love me.

I'm glad I've got this robe, but — guess what? — it hasn't made me perfect. It's the same body underneath the robe. I work with all the same struggles, fears, and angers all of us deal with. That's why sometimes the robe is dangerous, especially if we "wear" it all the time, because we need to know that we are flesh, that we are all in this together, that we are naked and human beneath our clothes.

The reason we sin and suffer is not so much because we are weak but simply because we are human. To be human means to be imperfect and in process. Thus I would define Christian maturity as the ability to joyfully live in an imperfect world. It's the only world we have.

The only reason evil bothers us — let's admit it — is because, for the most part, things are good. Mostly, things go right. That's why we get so upset at evil. Most days, these cells go on working, these eyes go on seeing, these ears keep hearing, while we're not doing much except shoving a little food into our mouth and everything keeps operating. Surely our foundational attitude needs to be gratitude. I like to call it an "attitude of gratitude."

The underlying and constant reality of our human existence is goodness.

In our moments of inspiration and insight and eucharist, we have to admit that somehow there is an amazing kind of grace at work and the very wonder of our existence boggles our minds. Yes, I exist, and I have existed long enough to complain. Then comes the question: Why should I even have a mouth to complain? Why should I be able to see the sky, the stars, or the faces of friends? I'm able *not* to enjoy only because I'm first able to enjoy.

Evil and sin are real and painful, but they are not decisive. That is what Christ came to teach us. I don't deny the reality of the world, the flesh, and the devil. All these bring evil into the world by the false promises they offer. They are real, but they are neither foundational nor final. Which leads us to what is final.

No dead end

The resurrection has been given to us as the final chapter of history. And put in the middle of the book to give us hope.

The cross is always *unto* resurrection. We've been told that in a thousand sermons, yet it is hard for us to believe. To believe in the resurrection is even a greater act of faith than to trust the pain of the cross.

It's as if God were holding up the crucifixion as a cosmic object lesson, and saying: "I know this is what you're experiencing, what you're in the middle of. Don't run from it. Learn from it, as I did. Hang there for a while, as I did. It will be your teacher. Rather than a losing of life, it is a gaining of life. It is the way through."

The human question when we are hanging there is first, "Why is my life like this?" (We all probably start there.) But grace leads us to an amazing and startling recognition, "My life is not about me." Think about that for the rest of your years. My life is not about me — this is the great and saving revelation that comes only from the whirlwind, and we are never ready for it.

It helps to remember that our suffering is not just for ourselves and not just about ourselves. Joyfully borne, suffering also helps other people. Redemptive suffering is, I believe, a radical call to deeper life and deeper faith that affects not only the self but others. I visit hospitals and see people suffering with resignation and even joy. Afterward, I feel my energy quadrupled. That's no small thing — the life we can share with others when we unite in the spirit of Christ's crucifixion and resurrection.

It's important that we become aware of this at least by our middle years. We are all moving toward old age, and the day is coming when suffering will be asked of each of us. Our suffering will be our opportunity to hand on life and strength to the world — to our children, our friends, and all those around us.

A time will come when, hopefully, the life of Christ will be so triumphant in us that we care more about others than about our own selves. Or better, when there is no longer such a sharp distinction between my self and their self. Remember that conversion is more than anything else *a reconstituted sense of the self.* My life is no longer just about me.

We should pray for the grace to bear our sufferings, whenever and however they come, as Christ bore his for us. Then we become crucified with Christ, as Paul described it. One of Paul's most eloquent passages is in Colossians (1:24): "It makes me happy to suffer for you as I am suffering now, and in my own body to do what I can to make up all that has still to be undergone by Christ for the sake of his body, the church." One could write a whole book on the theology locked up in that one sentence.

There is, in Paul's belief — and it underlies everything he writes about — a *real* unity between Christ and his members. We are not separate from him. We are his incarnation, his body. So our suffering is not separate; it is a continuation of the suffering of Christ that still endures for the life of the world. Much of Christianity has still not dealt with that. We still act as if Christ were "over there" and we are praying to Christ and pleasing Christ and trying to get Christ inside of us.

That's why I dislike such language as "I have accepted Christ into my heart as my personal savior." The implication is that we are actually separate and *our* brave decision changes all of that. The truth is that we are already in Christ by the power of the Spirit. We are his flesh, we are his body, we are his children. It's all a matter of recognition and response, which we call faith.

What does it mean to be a child of God? The human analogy helps. What was once inside the mother's womb is now outside, but our mother is still in us; we are still connected; we still have the same genes, the same DNA that we can never change. It's the same with God and his children. We frequently hear it said that baptism makes us children of God. Yes, but no. Baptism, rather, names the childhood that is already there.

All the children of the world are God's children. The thing is that some of them know it, and rejoice in it. Other people who never had water poured over their heads are also equally children of God. Some of them know it and act accordingly, and some of us who have been dunked neither believe nor behave accordingly.

Baptism, as Paul says, is a being dipped into the life, but also into the death. As the life of Christ is triumphant in us, the death of Christ is, too (Rom. 6:2–4). Christ is dying, Christ is living, Christ will come again — that is *the* basic mystery of faith that the Christian experiences, and it never stops. We are a continuation of the incarnation, a continuation of the passion and resurrection — we extend the whole life of Christ. History is a spiral led by grace, not a straight line led by logic. The true logic (*logos*) is the grace offered by Job and Jesus.

When we Christians begin to recognize the dignity we bear in our bodies, when we begin to know whose flesh we are, then we can begin to understand this moral life. We will not be acting for any finger-shaking reasons, not for reasons of ought or should, but simply letting the pattern of life and death live itself out within us. A new realm is offered here — the realm of grace.

Let love lead us on

We will not be weighing things in terms of good, better, best, but simply letting the life happen, letting the dying happen. And the reason we let suffering happen in us is because we let love lead us to its logical conclusion — which is that love gives itself away to the one it loves.

Sacrifice of oneself for the other is simply love in its later stages. It's a very old-fashioned word. We don't talk a lot about it anymore, but that's what love leads to. I don't see how we can show anybody we love them if we do not sacrifice for them.

This option for suffering should not be understood in a morbid sense. Our hurt of itself does not necessarily please

God, ourselves, or our neighbors. What is significant is the laying down of one's life for the sake of another.

Sacrifice comes from the words *sacrum facere*—to make sacred or holy. We make something holy by reconnecting it to the whole—in our case specifically by giving ourselves away to the other. A sacrifice does not mean that God is pleased by pain. It is, rather, a consecration by the self for the other, an offering of the self for the other. That, for some reason, is always convincing to human nature. When we go beyond the call of duty, when we lay our life down for our brother or sister, those for whom we make such a sacrifice are able to believe our love and believe that they can do the same. Thus redemptive suffering always generates immense life in others—that's why it's "redemptive."

Suffering, I believe, is sharing in the passion of God. For me, sometimes, that's the best way to say it: sharing in the passion of God. It is participating in what God is going through for the sake of love and union. It is the remending of a broken world, while paying the price for the mending thread ourselves.

I believe—if I am to believe Jesus—that God *is* suffering love. If we are created in God's image, and if there is this much suffering in the world, then God must also be suffering. How else can we understand the revelation of the cross?

Saved by a suffering God

Part of the reason people have so much trouble with this issue is because they think God is not suffering. Our definition of God has been inadequate. We envisioned God as complete and all-powerful and not suffering. But I think God is suffering, and when we suffer we are somehow in solidarity with God.

That may be why so many people who have suffered deeply are so holy. They have drawn close to God. It is the mystery of communion. Suffering is what God is going through to create life, and to maintain life. I don't know how to explain that — I haven't died yet, so I haven't seen God face to face or been told the answers. This is just an effort to draw together the wisdom of the centuries and a few insights from my own experience. This is how it seems to me to be happening, that's all.

This God who suffers the most is also the God who saves the most. The wounded one is the redeemer. Thus many cultures loved to picture Jesus as wounded from head to foot, and we thought the iconography was overdone. But it is exactly the same image with which we began this book: "Job was struck down with malignant ulcers from the sole of his foot to the top of his head" (2:8). He who carries all, understands all. He who has suffered all, has a universal compassion. He who has been afflicted and lived is the bearer of hope. *The wounded one is always the gift giver.* This is true in all the major stories of transformation and great religion.

Those who give their lives sacrificially, those willing to suffer with freedom and joy, are also those saving (however we may want to define that word) other people, liberating people more than anybody else.

Would there be communion at all if there were no need on this earth, no suffering on this earth? If there were no sin? No imperfection? I think there would be no such communion as we now have. We would each live in our isolated worlds. I would not need you. I would not be drawn to you. I would be self-sufficient. I would be caught up smugly and happily in my own perfection. I would simply draw my life totally from within and would never need to look at the beauty or pain on others' faces. This is the Gnostic temptation, condemned in some form in every century. There are two things that draw us outside of ourselves: pain on other people's faces; and the unbelievable beauty that is other human beings at their best. Or in other words: cross and resurrection.

Those — pain and beauty — constitute the two faces of

God. Unbelievable beauty, on the one hand, that we see reflected in the beauty of human beings to which we forever find ourselves attracted — whether it be physical beauty or spiritual beauty. But, on the other hand, mysteriously, brokenness, lameness, and weakness also pull us out of ourselves. We feel them both together in the case of a child. All a helpless child has to do is raise up its hands and most of us go rushing to help.

That factor of vulnerability forces us beyond ourselves. Whenever we see true pain, most of us are drawn out of our own preoccupations and want to take away the pain. I think we are rushing not just toward the hurt child, we are rushing toward God. Toward the suffering God. We want to take the suffering in our arms. That's why Francis could kiss the leper. That's why so many saints wanted to get near suffering — because, as they said again and again, they met Christ there. It "saved" them from their smaller and untrue self.

Many who are working among the suffering or poor say the same. They thought they were going as the benefactors, but they invariably found themselves being helped and liberated themselves. We are saved by those whom we go to save, and both of us are then saved in spite of ourselves. There is a mysterious "third" who is doing the saving. Suffering for and with the other seems to be the only way we know that our lives are not about us.

Epilogue

GOD IS LIGHT, yet this light seems to dwell in darkness. We must go into this darkness to see the light. Our age, however, resists the language of "descent." We belong to an age and culture that have been able to manufacture a kind of "ascent" unlike that of our ancestors. Reason, medicine, technology, and speed have allowed us to avoid the ordinary "path of the fall." Now we are unpracticed and afraid.

No piece of religious literature teaches the way of descent more daringly and effectively than the Book of Job. Even the name Job is considered by some linguists to be an acronym for "Where is the Father?" The name and the story cry out against a darkness that refuses to reveal itself — and a path that does not at first feel like life at all.

Surely no book is less an answer book than the Book of Job. No book is less therapeutic or less "helpful," as we ordinarily use the term. It fixes nothing, explains nothing, and dismisses those who even try to explain. Surely it is amazing that anyone dared to write or publish such a book. Or that we bother to read it. It shows all the signs of authentic divine revelation, but reveals hardly anything that we first hoped for. Yet the story of Job realigns and regenerates the soul in ways that few books can. One must ask why.

If the postmodern crisis is above all else a crisis of the self, and I think it is, the story of Job realigns the self correctly and truthfully. It is the truth that saves us, much more than mere sincerity, hard work, or religious practice. What both Job and Jesus seem to say is that truth is finally a person and an encounter — much more than a concept that can be argued. We are realigned with truth when the real person meets the real God — which is exactly the stuff of spirituality, theology, and conversion.

It is not quick or easy, we find, to allow the true self or to allow the true God. The task of life is the gradual unveiling of both, an unveiling that is as savage and as sacred as this perilous descent of Job. Remember, the descent took forty-one chapters, the ascent not even one. Resurrection takes care of itself. It comes naturally once the false self is abandoned. But what an abandoning! Every movement toward union will feel like a loss of self-importance and self-control.

The restored Job and the risen Christ are images of the substantial self, no longer private, separate, or autonomous, but hidden in God. The true self is not lost in a transitory house of mirrors, but founded in the unreflected and perfect Reflector we all long for: "And from my flesh I shall look on God" (19:26). All we need to know is that God is looking back — and not away from our gaze.

Lest the subplot be missed in the wonder of seeing and being seen, we must not overlook the radical critique of religion that also emerges from the Book of Job. All our usual religious responses are judged worthy of God's anger at his people "for not having spoken correctly about me" (42:7).

Imagine God saying that about religious ideology, orthodoxy, conventional wisdom, and heroic idealism. Yet these are the ever-so-close masquerades and substitutes for authentic faith that characterize the four good friends. They are dangerous precisely because they are "friends" — so close, so common, so connected to the real thing.

But if that is not enough, this penultimate statement of faith in the Hebrew scriptures is readily attributed to a Gentile. It is surely a sign of both divine inspiration and ultimate self-criticism that the Jewish people dared to include it among their canonical writings at all. They are assuring us, against all attempts at institutional idolatry, that faith can forever be found, like the hill of Calvary, "outside the walls." In fact, that is where it finds its most ready soil — at the bottom, the broken, the edges of things.

If no meaning can be given to human suffering, if our wounds are not capable of becoming sacred wounds, the human project is surely doomed to a blaming war of all against all. The future would then be full of scapegoats and victims. This is no peripheral question the Book of Job pursues. In fact, it might well be the question on which both faith and human history rise and fall.

Without the answer from the whirlwind, the coming century will surely be "nasty, brutish, and short" for most people. There will be no place to go to make our wounds sacred, but they will still be wounds, sore and bleeding. Without Job and Jesus, our only remaining question is "*who* is to blame for my unhappiness?" It is the predictable and perennial question of Satan, the "accuser."

If there is no voice from the whirlwind, no calming eyes in the heart of the tempest, humanity can only "sit on its dungheap picking at its sores."

But we — we few, I'm afraid — have heard a story that is always true. A story that makes all our wounds sacred.

Artist's Interpretation of the Illustrations

Page 12: Job's portrait including opposites: young and old, rich and imprisoned (bars), blessed with beauty

Page 22: Existence and faith; a partition line: a man paces protecting his eyes out of a foreboding, while he is still caught up in worldly affairs; at the same time another gropes into the void through faith up toward the light.

Page 38: God's seed and the fruit of life.

Page 51: The roots are entangled in the stones...

Page 71: A human being is only full of words.

Page 87: Encounter and retort, the servant Job facing God or Satan.

Page 114–15: A human being, demystified by knowledge, crushed by information, in doubt about hope and faith.

Page 129: Yearning; my soul is dissolving within me — you don't answer.

Page 151: God's eye: veiled for us — but it watches over human activities.

Page 170: Human shadows, bodies disappear, words and memories remain.

Page 184: Encounter and reconciliation with God.

About the artist...

PATRICIA KARG
academic sculptress and painter

"Through my pictures and sculptures
I want to uplift and expand the human spirit.
My work is meant to be nourishment for the soul."

Born in Innsbruck, Austria, in 1961

1976–1980: college for wood and stone carving in Innsbruck; successfully completed in 1980

1980–1987: study of sculpture at the Academy of Fine Arts in Munich; diploma, master scholar of Prof. Ladner

International exhibitions since 1980

Prizes and Awards:

1981	Prize of the International Summer Academy in Innsbruck
1983	Prize awarded by the Town of Innsbruck
	Prize of the International Summer Academy
1984	Prize of the 88th German Catholic Congress, Munich
1986	1st Prize redesign of parish church, St. Philip Neri, Munich
1987	Prize awarded by the Town of Innsbruck for painting; topic: Peace
1988	Award for Small Work by the International Art Competition, New York
	Prize for painting awarded by the Town of Innsbruck
1992	1st Prize for the "Hahnenkamm-Poster"
	1st Prize for "Datecom" Art Competition
1993	3rd Prize, Creation of Barbara's Bridge in Schwaz

Many public works

Address: Patricia Karg
Schossgasse 10A
A-6065 Thaur
Austria

Richard Rohr, O.F.M., is a Franciscan of the New Mexico Province. He was founder of the New Jerusalem Community in Cincinnati, Ohio, and the Center for Action and Contemplation in Albuquerque, New Mexico. After thirteen years as pastor of New Jerusalem and eight years as animator of the Center in Albuquerque, he handed them both over to lay leadership and direction.

Richard now lives in a Franciscan community in New Mexico and divides his public time between local work and preaching and teaching around the world.

Richard was born in Topeka, Kansas, in 1943. He entered the Franciscan Order in 1961 and was ordained to the priesthood in 1970. He received his Master's Degree in Theology from the University of Dayton and did advanced study in Scripture at the University of Notre Dame and the University of San Francisco.

Also by Richard Rohr:

DISCOVERING THE ENNEAGRAM
An Ancient Tool for a New Spiritual Journey
0-8245-1185-9 $12.95 pb 272 pages

ENNEAGRAM II
Advancing Spiritual Discernment
0-8245-1451-3 $17.95 hc 204 pages

EXPERIENCING THE ENNEAGRAM
0-8245-1201-4 $13.95 pb 228 pages

QUEST FOR THE GRAIL
Soul Work and the Sacred Journey
O-8245-1411-4 $17.95 hc 160 pages

SIMPLICITY
The Art of Living
0-8245-1251-0 $11.95 pb 180 pages

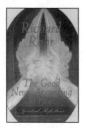